SCM STUDYGUIDE
TO LITURGY

Stephen Burns

scm press

Scripture quotations are from the New Revised Standard Version of the Bible, copyright 1989 by the Division of Christian Education of the National Council of the Churches of Christ in the USA. Used by permission. All rights reserved.

British Library Cataloguing in Publication data

A catalogue record for this book is available from the British Library

0 334 04013 2/
9780 334 04013 2

First published in 2006 by SCM Press
9–17 St Albans Place
London N1 0NX

www.scm-canterburypress.co.uk

SCM Press is a division of
SCM-Canterbury Press Ltd

Printed and bound in Great Britain by
Creative Print and Design, Wales

Contents

Contents

Preface

There are different ways to approach the study of liturgy. For example, much liturgical study has a strongly historical emphasis, concerned with uncovering ancient texts, reconstructing their setting and contextualizing their content in their theological and wider cultural milieux. Such an approach usually involves a strong textual emphasis because, of course, it is the written forms of prayers, rather than extemporized prayers, which are recoverable. No serious study of liturgical developments can or ought to undervalue this kind of textual and contextual work; however, awareness that prayer is extemporized as well as written is itself a reminder that a textual focus and a historical approach are not, nor should be, the whole of liturgical study. While the concerns of textual, historical trajectories are by no means jettisoned in this book, it sets about to study liturgy with a wider view which acknowledges extemporized and non-verbal dimensions of worship. It attempts not only to take the non-verbal dimensions of worship seriously in those traditions that do employ written texts in their worship, but also to embrace those traditions that do not. This is one dimension of its ecumenical scope.

The book begins with a focus on 'participation' and ends by reflecting on presidency. Although it will be of particular interest to those who lead worship, it is intended as a book for all who engage in liturgy. Its central conviction is that the multidimensional notion of 'participation' is fundamental to liturgy; indeed, it is very close to liturgy's core meaning as 'people's work'. The book celebrates the ways in which participation requires involvement by all and not just specialist expertise by leaders, however important that also may be.

Nurturing participation in worship is a key concern of the Liturgical Movement as it seeks the renewal of the churches' worship. This book is strongly
committed to the vision, and promotes the perspectives, of the movement. So
it is intended as a study oriented to celebration, which yields ideas and offers
resources that can be put to practice in gatherings of the church. It draws
on texts and other aspects of worship from a range of churches' resources
for worship, and it is deeply indebted to others engaged in the ecumenical
quest to serve the worship of the church. The wisdom, prayers, questions,
critiques and aspirations of a wide range of liturgical leaders and scholars
are scattered through this book, sometimes presented directly in quotation,
always informing my own modest thought.

As well as enabling ecumenical sharing, the Liturgical Movement has been
vigorously engaged with the many missionary challenges that the churches
face in the modern world, seeking to foster an outward-looking attitude
and hospitality in Christian assemblies. Both the ecumenical and missionary concerns of liturgical renewal are, I hope, present on every page of this
book, and the two main parts of the book reflect these two priorities. Part 1,
'Shaping Christian Worship', takes an ecumenical perspective on the range of
activities and resources that determine Christian worship. The titles of the
four chapters in Part 1 are self-evident: 'Scripture and Sacrament' (Chapter
1), 'Space and Symbol' (Chapter 2), 'Music and Song' (Chapter 3) and
'Discipleship and Learning: The Sermon' (Chapter 4). Part 2, 'Worship and
Mission in a Diverse World', celebrates the rich and robust ways in which the
liturgy responds to human need. Chapter 5 explores the substance of various
styles of worship, particularly feeling the weight of a range of contemporary
challenges to ecumenical liturgical convergence: 'alternative worship', the
charismatic tradition, feminist, gay and lesbian and postcolonial perspectives
are among the things considered. Chapter 6 introduces cycles of liturgical
time and touches on the crises of the human life-cycle to which liturgy ministers. Among the foci of the chapter are the particular features of seasons of
the Christian year, and the potential for pastoral care in the seven sacraments
of the Catholic tradition. Chapter 7 considers various ways in which worship
nurtures human maturity and helps the fullness of life to flourish.

Throughout the book, I have made hard choices about what to cover
and what to leave aside. Its final contents reflect my convictions about what

participants and presiders most need to think about to engage the renewal of worship, its ecumenical scope and its missionary potential. But, of course, even of the topics that the book does cover, much more might be said. Therefore, at the end of each chapter, suggestions for further reading point to studies that develop ideas that this present book only introduces. One of the priorities it does reflect is to introduce, alongside the best of the British literature, the wealth of North American liturgical theology which is as yet little known in Britain.

The Studyguide arises out of my teaching at the Queen's Foundation for Ecumenical Theological Education in Birmingham. It most closely relates to the course Liturgical Theology and Practice which I have taught for four years now, and which has allowed me to share with and learn from many students preparing for public ministry in three ecclesial traditions: the Church of England, the Methodist Church and the United Reformed Church. Although the book's ecumenical range of reference is much wider, it makes special mention of the contemporary resources of these three traditions (that is, to *Common Worship: Services and Prayers for the Church of England*, the *Methodist Worship Book* and *Worship from the United Reformed Church*), and also to the Baptist Union's *Gathering for Worship* which, with the three just mentioned, is the other major recent publication of a prayerbook among the British churches.

I am indebted to numerous students and colleagues at the Queen's Foundation for their encouragement as I wrote this book. I must make particular mention of Nicola Slee whose affirmation was crucial, especially at the early stages of the project; Michael Jagessar, whose shared work with me on developing a postcolonial perspective on liturgy is included in Chapter 5; Andy Lyons, who is a valued conversation partner about liturgical matters; and David Hewlett, without whose support this book would never have appeared. Beyond Queen's, I am grateful for conversation about this book with bishops Stephen Platten and David Stancliffe, and I continue to be immensely grateful to Ann Loades and Richard Giles for all that they have taught me, although of course none of those I mention are in any way responsible for the weaknesses of my rigour or vision in the pages of this book. I also owe thanks to Christine Smith and Barbara Laing at SCM-Canterbury Press for commissioning and overseeing this project.

Copyright acknowledgement and notes on permission to use particular prayers, poems and songs are found at the end of the book. In seeking permissions, I was glad to make new contacts and am grateful for both consent to use copyrighted material and interest in this project.

Above all I am grateful to Judith for everything. Dominic was born in the middle of preparing this Studyguide – and he is a delight to us both. Every day he has given reason for our thanks and praise.

Finally, this book is dedicated to Joyce and Bruce Hunn, whose friendship is a treasure.

Introduction

Participating in Liturgy

What is liturgy?
What does participation in liturgy require?

In his novel *Il Postino*, Antonio Skarmeta tells a story of life among the handful of inhabitants on a remote island, Isla Negra. One of the islanders is the notable poet Pablo Neruda, who lives in a villa high on the mountainside, overlooking the ocean. Another is Mario Jiminez, the postman from whom the novel takes its name. Mario, like most of the islanders, is illiterate, and Pablo Neruda is in fact the only person for miles around to receive mail with any regularity. Mario therefore has plenty of opportunity to meet him, and plenty of time on his hands to daydream. And most of his daydreams are about a girl, Beatriz Gonzalez, a waitress in her family's tavern on the waterfront of the local port.

Mario wants to find a way to woo Beatriz, and his pursuit of her is the heart of the novel. Mario asks Neruda to help him seduce Beatriz. He wants him to teach him poetry, so that he can draw her attention and impress her with metaphor: one of his first attempts is '[your] smile stretches across [your] face like a butterfly'![1] And, as the story unfolds, she does fall for him, with Neruda becoming the best man at the couple's wedding.

Although essentially a love story, the novel is set in the wider context of political upheaval in Neruda's native Chile. So, as well as falling in love, Mario receives an education in politics, and Neruda himself returns to the mainland to fight in the cause of communism. One day, from Chile, Neruda writes to Mario (now able to read) and asks him to make a tape recording of sounds from around the island. Mario sets determinedly about his task, taking an old Sony spool recorder and microphone around with him. He climbs a bell tower and captures the sound of the wind blowing through it, then of him clanging the large bell. He stands on the beach, holding the microphone out to the ocean to record the noise of waves hitting the rocks and then of 'the sea retreating'.[2] He tapes gulls flapping their wings along the water's edge, the buzzing hum of a beehive, various birds singing, dogs barking at night, and finally, the crying of Beatriz and his newborn baby, named Don Pablo after Neruda, and who the poet has not yet seen.

The film version of *Il Postino* is an especially delightful and detailed portrayal of Mario at this task. We see him giving careful attention to identify the sounds that surround Isla Negra, then taking considerable care to capture them on tape. He strains to relate the magic of the island, its particular features and distinctive things . . .

Paying Attention to Christian Worship

Now, the point of my beginning with a story that never mentions worship is that I want to suggest that Mario's sound-recording is a marvellous image to transport into the start of our thinking about liturgy. To describe worship in a particular place, with a specific congregation, Mario can help us. Imagining your regular experience of worship as your 'island':

- What might you want to record to convey a sense of it?
- What is characteristic or impressive about a particular service, or your congregation?
- What makes your liturgy distinctive?
- What are the riches of your tradition?
- What are the sounds of your worship?

Perhaps above all, Mario's tape-recording reminds us of the difference between words and sounds. He does not describe the island – he records it. Similarly, liturgy is more than words on a page, more than texts from prayerbooks (or sometimes, PowerPoint projectors). Liturgy is at least the sounds of those texts spoken, apart from all kinds of other details, both sonic and relating to the other senses. As the preface to the *Methodist Worship Book* (1999) puts it: 'worship is not a matter of words alone. It involves not only what we say but also what we do';[3] or even more succinctly, the Church of England's *New Patterns for Worship* (2002) has as its opening words: 'Worship is not worship until you do it.'[4] Liturgy is not the same as books, however important books may be to particular styles of celebration. The liturgy is something bigger than texts or words – certainly something more sensual – involving hearing, sight, smell, taste and touch.[5]

Note that if we want to speak about a particular act of worship on a given occasion, simply to say that, for example, 'the liturgy followed *Worship from the United Reformed Church* (2003)', or '. . . followed *Common Worship* (2000)' yields very little detail. Many congregations of the Church of England will have used *Common Worship* and their worship will have been remarkably diverse. Many congregations of the United Reformed Church will have referred to their new prayerbook, but their use of it may have been extraordinarily varied from place to place.

In this Studyguide, we are looking to Mario to learn to see worship in a more nuanced way.

Engaging the Senses

The non-textual dimensions of worship are of enormous importance. Words from a page may be spoken or sung, either by a single voice, or by a range of voices in unison. Words are 'layered', as it were. Additionally, singing voices may well be accompanied by different kinds of music, adding another kind of depth to the human voice. Worship unavoidably involves other kinds of audible noises – footsteps, perhaps the pouring of water or wine – but other kinds of noise may have also been integral to liturgy: in many congregations, noise such as handclapping, a human contribution – like the voice – accompanied by, or accompanying, music.

Sighted people are likely to find the visual dimension of worship most significant, even though liturgical books may say little explicitly about the 'staging' of visual aspects of liturgy. The human face is central to visual engagement in worship – a communal experience, worship involves other people, and particular faces (of ministers or worship leaders) may be especially prominent. Human figures may also be depicted in glass, stone or woodwork, in painting or embroidery. Signs and symbols – not least, the cross – may also be important aspects of the worship environment which worshippers have in their sight. This list of things seen in worship might be extended, extensively.

Other senses may not always be so engaged, but the taste of bread and wine in the sharing of holy communion is likely to be a valued dimension of the experience of worship for many people. Touch may be a regular part of the proceedings of liturgy: some of it shared among just some of the people present – hands laid upon others in gestures of blessing or commissioning, for instance – while other touch is likely to be shared more widely, such as in 'the sign of peace' when the service fragments for the purpose of greeting the presence of each one assembled. In some traditions, use of incense will be an obvious part of how the sense of smell is engaged in worship, honouring holy things or accompanying the prayer of the saints in the local congregation, but more subtly, smell may have been significant for others in other ways: the aroma of cut flowers, noted on the anniversary of a member of the congregation lost in death. Or, indeed, the smell of good coffee brewing in the background ready for the end of the liturgy may be a most helpful signal of a welcome place of hospitality.

In fact, the sensual dimensions of worship are only one of the ways in which worship is bodily, or embodied. Movement may be significant in liturgy, with processions of people perhaps marking important moments – such as the movement of the scriptures to the centre of the assembly, as a symbol of Christ at the heart of the church.

Postures may also be important to people's sense of worship: standing in confidence, kneeling in reverence, raising hands in thanksgiving, or signing the self with the mark of the cross, as ways of enacting prayer.

Relatively recently, liturgical scholarship has begun to attend to the embodied and sensual dimensions of liturgy in such a way as to make the study of worship less fixated with 'dissecting, reducing, analyzing, [and] abstracting' texts.[6] It is a central conviction of this book that liturgy is necessarily concerned with this more expansive agenda, and not simply with texts alone.

The Meaning of 'Liturgy'

Worship, then, is so much more than words, and 'liturgy' should be used to include this 'so much more'. It can be immensely helpful to remember that the word 'liturgy' means something like 'people's work' (from the Greek words *laos*, 'people', and *ergon*, 'work'), which at the very least suggests that liturgy is not principally about a prayerbook. In fact, although Christian liturgy will inevitably use the Bible, sometimes in some places, and much of the time in others, no other book (than the Bible) is used in a service of worship.

In order to stop equating liturgy with texts it is, of course, worth understanding at least something of how the confusion between the two arose. An association between liturgy and text emerged in the medieval period and was further made possible by the invention of the printing press.[7] This was congenial to the churches for all sorts of reasons: it made possible the printing of Bibles as well as prayerbooks, and enabled both Roman and Protestant Christians to impose conformity in many matters of liturgy. For example, a single form of words was published for the celebration of the mass in the first Book of Common Prayer (1549) of the Church of England: the book declared that 'from henceforth, all the whole realm shall have but one use'. Many of the Reformers in their turn imposed a single order for the celebration of worship in the traditions they were crafting, in contradistinction from the Roman forms they were defining themselves against, which were also increasingly standardized. Restricting what was said to words on a page was, on all sides, about preserving and nurturing good doctrine – 'orthodoxy' – however that was understood.

The legacy of this text-based concentration in liturgy is so powerful that the study of liturgy has, historically, largely been a matter of examining texts – either those of very ancient provenance, or those recovered from particular periods of controversy. The relatively recent move in liturgical study to focus some attention outside this strong textual emphasis has accompanied a contemporary mood in both the Roman and Protestant traditions that has regarded standardization as problematic and undesirable. And just as the initial medieval shift towards standardization was partly related to technological change (the printing press), contemporary diversification is partly related to modern-day media (such as computer technology).

More than this, however, a contemporary unease with standardization in liturgy has been influenced by the pluralism in which liberal societies best flourish. Particularly significant is our growing awareness of the damage caused by imperialism (by which powerful cultures have imposed their assumptions and values, quite disastrously, upon others). Guardedness about the risks of imperialism has properly informed the 'inculturation' of liturgical forms, and 'liturgical inculturation' has sought to engage closely with the localities, societies and subcultures in which Christian worship is celebrated, and has led to the reshaping of the style and content of worship so as to reflect the particularities of local situations.

This leads us to something else that is often much misunderstood: the distinction between 'liturgical' and 'non-liturgical' forms of worship. The idea of a gathering for 'non-liturgical' worship is in fact a misnomer, a contradiction in terms – at least, it is if the people are involved in the 'work' of worship. This means at least that liturgy is not something 'done' by a presiding minister before an observing congregation: for liturgy is 'people's work'. An adequate understanding of liturgy needs to emphasize all the people, and the range of roles played by various people, and not just the presiding person, or a prescriptive or ancient text. It has a much bigger scope, and it leads us to the emphatic weight given in liturgical studies to the notion of 'participation'.

Participation as the First Principle of Christian Worship

At the heart of good liturgy is an idea enshrined in the meaning of 'liturgy' itself. For at least 40 years or so, the language of 'participation' has been widely used by the churches as key to what liturgy, as 'people's work', is and ought to be. A classic expression of the aspiration of participation in liturgy is the fourteenth paragraph of *Sacrosanctum concilium*, the liturgy document of the Second Vatican Council of the Roman Catholic Church:

Mother Church earnestly desires that all the faithful should be led to that full, conscious, and active participation in liturgical celebrations which is demanded by the very nature of the liturgy, and to which the Christian people, 'a chosen race, a royal priesthood, a holy nation, a redeemed people' (1 Pet. 2.9; cf 4–5) have a right and obligation by reason of their baptism. In the restoration and promotion of the sacred liturgy the full, conscious and active participation by all the people is the aim to be considered before all else, for it is the primary and indispensable source from which the faithful are to derive the true Christian spirit. Therefore, in all their apostolic activity, pastors of souls should energetically set about achieving it through requisite pedagogy . . .'[8]

While the Second Vatican Council has sometimes been regarded as the most important thing to affect Protestantism in the twentieth century,[9] this particular statement from it, about 'participation' in liturgy, is likewise regarded as 'an ecumenical treasure'.[10] This emphasis on participation certainly shapes the orders of worship in the recently published prayerbooks of diverse traditions, such as *The Methodist Worship Book* (1999), *Common Worship: Services and Prayers for the Church of England* (2000), *Worship from the United Reformed Church* (2003) and the Baptist Union's *Gathering for Worship: Patterns and Prayers for the Community of Disciples* (2005). This fact is very quickly borne out by reference to the books, each of which echoes Vatican II on the centrality of participation. Among the first words of the *Methodist Worship Book*, we find the claim that 'worship is the work of the whole people of God: a congregation is not an audience or group of spectators. Those who lead worship are called to encourage, and with the help of the Holy Spirit, to enable the whole body of Christ to participate fully'.[11] Similarly, the first words of *Common Worship* speak of the 'challenge to draw the whole community of the people we serve into the worship of God'.[12] Furthermore, one of the stated aims of the new orders of service for holy communion in the United Reformed Church is that 'a greater degree of participation by the congregation is allowed for, both in the responses and in physical movement'.[13]

The *Methodist Worship Book*'s stress that the congregation is not an audience resonates with a comparison made by the eighteenth-century Danish Lutheran philosopher Søren Kierkegaard, who in his writings compared worship to the theatre. The staging of a play, he suggested, involves three groups of people: actors, who perform; promptors, who enable the actors to perform well; and the audience, who listen and observe. Kierkegaard made the point that many of his Christian contemporaries might make the analogy between worship and theatre like this: the clergy or leaders are the actors, God is the clergy's prompter, and the congregation is the audience, watching – and judging – the clergy's performance. Kierkegaard argued that such an understanding is profoundly mistaken and, rather, the whole congregation are the 'actors' in worship, the clergy role is analogous to the actors' promptors, helping them to perform as best as possible, and the audience is God! God is the one before whom the whole congregation enacts worship.[14]

The Roman Catholic liturgist Gabe Huck comments on the key phrase in paragraph 14 of *Sacrosanctum concilium*, on 'full, conscious and active participation', in such a way as it make the main point even plainer: 'it is the nature of the liturgy to be done by people. It is not done to people. It is not done for people. It is not done in the presence of people. People do it and the plural is correct because it is as a Church assembled that people do liturgy.'[15] This is the central conviction which the Protestant churches have absorbed from the 'ecumenical treasure' of Vatican II, and so understanding the centrality of participation to the vision of contemporary service books in countless traditions is essential to celebrating the services they contain.

It is worth noting that further comments from Gabe Huck's reflections on *Sacrosanctum concilium* 14 challengingly introduce criteria about the assessment of worship: 'a liturgy has not "worked" simply because people leave uplifted, made peaceful, made cheerful, made warm, made smarter, or all of the above'.[16] His point is, simply, that worship has 'worked' if people have participated, and this is the criteria that leaders and congregations need to use as their primary measure. There are obvious alliances here with Kierkegaard's, and the Methodists', comment that the congregation is not an audience.

Aspects of Participation

As we can see that the importance of participation is widely affirmed, it also becomes possible to appreciate the beginnings of an agenda for liturgical study. Most obviously, we have an imperative for forms and occasions of worship to be participatory, to the best possible degree; less obvious, perhaps, is the need for a sense of the subtleties of participation. For it might be assumed that the language of participation suggests a certain style of worship, more 'loud' than 'still', perhaps, or more 'lively' than 'reverent'. However, one of the things that liturgical scholarship since Vatican II has explored is the multi-textured nature of participation.

So participation might, for some, mean banging a tamborine, but it will almost certainly always also involve a capacity for quietude and for spacious reflection. 'Participation' is more complex than it might at first seem, and studies of participation have become increasingly subtle. In the remaining part of this Introduction, then, we consider three scholarly contributions to exploration of participation in liturgy, which we will carry with us into the rest of the book. First, the Methodist liturgist James White points to a number of areas 'beyond the words that are said and sung', and appeals for attention to a quite lengthy list of things to which participation relates:

> Who the people are (age, race, sex), what roles each group plays (includ-ing the ordained clergy and choir), what is the architectural setting of the worship, what visual arts are present, how people arrive and leave, what actions happen (such as offering, receiving communion, baptism, etc.), what leadership roles are apparent (usher, reader, presider), who sings and how, the uses of music, the use or not of printed materials, use of the body (handclapping, hands raised), and how strangers are treated.[17]

As a prominent lecturer on Christian worship in American universities, White has developed this particular list for use with his students, and it is the kind of thing that, over time, will hopefully provide pathways out of the narrow focus on texts with which much university teaching on worship has been limited, in the USA and elsewhere. The image of Mario taping sounds around his island echoes the vision and kinds of wide foci of attention that White and others highlight and helps to redress the narrow and limiting imbalance of concentration on texts alone.

If White's list is a starting point to developing sensitivity to the textures of worship, we can expand his vision by referring to some other liturgical theo-logians. As our second example, then, the Roman Catholic liturgist David

Power distinguishes different 'levels of meaning' in a worship event, and his stress on the various *understandings* of worship among those who take part in it provides an interesting *internal* emphasis that sits alongside White's list of things that might be observed *externally*. In this, then, we have a significantly thickened sense of the subtlety of participation. Power suggests that three kinds of meaning can be distinguished in an event of worship: 'First, there is the meaning that the ritual has when it is taken as a text within a tradition, with a potential to be appropriated'. This is the level at which, as we have said, so much of the study of liturgy has begun and ended, without going further. Power, however, does go further: 'there is . . . also the meaning that is given to the ritual by the participants when they employ it to refer to their own world of reference, one which may not be coterminous with the traditional sense of the ritual'. Here, he indicates that personal meanings found in worship may diverge from 'official' understandings, perhaps in terms of denominational statements of belief or in relation to the explanations of theologians immersed in the long histories of development in worship practice. As Power observes, this potential divergence has a number of impacts: on 'the organic growth of the ritual and the ways in which it is passed on, to what moments of life it belongs, in what circumstances it is celebrated', and so on. And there is then a third level of meaning that emerges in the difference between 'the meaning which may be given to the ritual by the official church representative and that which is given by the other participants'. An official representative, perhaps most obviously a presiding minister, may have a very different perception of a worship event than others involved in it.

There is much to think about in Power's description of the meanings of worship: there are at least the meanings brought to or derived from the worship event by the presiding minister, the other people involved, and the 'authoritative' persons compiling or commenting on texts and traditions employed in the act of worship. Discerning these different levels of meanings is, of course, by no means easy, as perhaps much of the time they are constantly interacting. However, Power's criteria illuminate how rich a description of worship it may be possible to gain when people are able to express and be articulate about their experience of liturgy.[18]

Reference at this point to one more liturgical theologian might illuminate one of the levels of meanings to which Power points, and will also anticipate some of the themes we shall explore later in the book. Marjorie Procter-Smith is an Anglican (Episcopalian) theologian (who teaches at a Methodist seminary) who has developed some distinctively feminist approaches to liturgical study. When she writes about 'praying between the lines', we have an instance of Power's second level of meaning – that given to it by participants which may not cohere with 'official' understandings of what the liturgy expresses. Because the production of liturgy, presidency in liturgy, and study of and commentary upon liturgy has largely been a male enterprise, Procter-Smith is aware that women's voices and women's perspectives have often not been incorporated into 'official' liturgies. Rather, official liturgical resources have tended to be dominated by the experience and perspectives of men. For Procter-Smith and others, 'praying between the lines' is a way of 'translating as we go, reading ourselves into the text from which we have been excised, by reading behind the texts, reading the silences and the spaces, the absences and omissions'. In so doing, she says, 'we learn to hear words not spoken aloud, see signs unread by others'. For many women, and some men, this kind of approach to worship is essential as 'a strategy of survival and resistance', a means by those who do so of protecting themselves from further exclusion, and of resisting the possibility of further exclusion. Much of the 'praying between the lines' that goes on among feminists and others is, in Procter-Smith's word, 'internal', that is, unspoken. But on occasion, it might be voiced. Perhaps especially when such prayer is voiced, Procter-Smith's main point becomes most evident: that 'although univocal prayer claims to speak for all, the existence of different "translations" of one univocal prayer makes it clear that it does not. Current "unison" or 'corporate' prayer is in fact not "accessible to every individual"; it is not in fact one voice, one body, but many voices, many bodies, many of whom are praying between the lines'.[19] As an example of one of the levels of meaning to which David Power points us, Marjorie Procter-Smith presents a very serious challenge to students of liturgy to look beyond the 'official' texts for prayer.

As liturgical renewal and revision continues over the coming years, it will become more and more important that worshipping congregations engage with perspectives like Marjorie Procter-Smith's. Feminist, postcolonialist and other theological perspectives sensitive and alert to dynamics of exclusion will rightly become more prominent in liturgical study.

Back to the Beginning

Our opening image of Mario recording sounds perhaps now seems more complex. Paying close attention to liturgy is not as charming as it may at first have appeared, with Mario falling in love in the balmy heat of summer. Starting with Mario, we have gone on to acknowledge that liturgy involves many things, that its core concepts involve considerable subtlety, and that the ways it is crafted, celebrated and controlled have power to include or exclude. Subsequent chapters of this book will explore these issues in increasing detail. For the time being, we can appreciate that careful awareness of liturgy requires strained effort to notice things that might otherwise be overlooked, very careful discernment, and the negotiation of numerous power-games.

Further Reading

Paul Bradshaw (ed.), *The New SCM Dictionary of Liturgy and Worship* (London: SCM Press, 2002).

John Fenwick and Bryan Spinks, *Worship in Transition: The Twentieth Century Liturgical Movement* (Edinburgh: T & T Clark, 1995).

Peter Fink (ed.), *The New Dictionary of Sacramental Worship* (Collegeville, MN: Liturgical Press, 1992).

Cheslyn Jones, Edward Yarnold, Geoffrey Wainwright and Paul Bradshaw (eds), *The Study of Liturgy* (London: SPCK, 1992).

Jean Lebon, *How to Understand the Liturgy* (London: SCM Press, 1987).

Keith Pecklers, *Worship* (London: Continuum, 2003).

Don E. Saliers, *Worship as Theology: Foretaste of Glory Divine* (Nashville, TN: Abingdon Press, 1994).

Dwight W. Vogel, *Primary Sources of Liturgical Theology: A Reader* (Collegeville, MN: Liturgical Press, 2000).

James F. White, *Documents of Christian Worship: Descriptive and Interpretive Sources* (Edinburgh: T & T Clark, 1994).

James F. White, *Introduction to Christian Worship* (Nashville, TN: Abingdon Press, 2000).

Susan J. White, *Groundwork of Christian Worship* (Peterborough: Epworth Press, 1997).

Part 1

Shaping Christian Worship

Throughout the first main part of this book we explore the basic elements of Christian worship: Chapter 1 considers scripture and sacrament, and Chapters 2–4 consider, in turn, space and symbol, music and song, and preaching. We can think of these as the various 'building blocks' that are assembled together in liturgy. Although the same materials are used, the structures can be varied. It is not that each of these elements is equal, for the Christian theological tradition has viewed some more consciously than others, given greater weight to some, made some more central.

Throughout the first part of the book we constantly recall another image, that of bones and flesh, to suggest that scripture and sacrament provide the essential framework of Christian liturgy, the skeleton, which other aspects of liturgy then enflesh, wrap around and form the shape of Christian worship.

1

Scripture and Sacrament

What are the biblical roots of the service of word and table?
In addition to Bible readings, how else is scripture present in liturgy?
Apart from stories of the last supper, what else is important in a biblical
*   understanding of holy communion?*
What is the shape of eucharistic prayer?

The Bible and the sacraments of baptism and holy communion can rightly
be regarded as the 'bones' of Christian worship. Pursuing the anatomical
analogy, they are the skeletal elements around which Christian liturgies are
enfleshed. Throughout this chapter, we explore the ways in which scripture
and sacraments provide the basic shape of the liturgy; how they are central
to making Christian worship what it is.

Biblical Grounds of Christian Worship

It has been a key concern of recent liturgical renewal to impress the centrality
of scripture and sacrament, but it can also be argued that their importance is
as ancient as the faith itself. Within the scriptures, we find various testimonies
to their presence in Christian worship. These scriptural testimonies give us
little detail of what early Christian worship may have been like, but they do
suggest that scripture, baptism and eucharist all played a role. A 'classic' reference is the Lucan story of the Emmaus road. Note that, in the story, the risen
Jesus opens the scriptures to the disciples: 'beginning with Moses and all the

prophets, Jesus interpreted to them the things about himself in all the scriptures' (Luke 24.27); and later, at table, as they shared a meal: 'they recognized him in the breaking of bread' (Luke 24.35). Even if this story is the historical account of a particular occasion, of course it was not the case that the Risen One had in his hands a bound copy of the books of the Bible like our own 'scripture', and neither was the meal shared a service of 'holy communion'. But, nevertheless, we do find a hint that, in some sense, the story of our scriptures and the first germs of a distinctive kind of table-companionship are embedded in the narrative, perhaps reflecting the Lucan community's own habit of reading and telling the story of the Emmaus road when gathered for a simple meal at which they searched the scriptures.

Luke leaves us some other clues about the presence of scripture and sacrament in the church's worship in the earliest days. In the Acts of the Apostles, he gives a concentrated account of the new community: 'they devoted themselves to the apostles' teaching and fellowship, to the breaking of bread and the prayers' (Acts 2.42). As with the Emmaus tradition, 'the apostles' teaching' is not to be equated with the four canonical Gospels that became the core of the Christian inheritance – for, of course, Acts predates the distinct authority the Gospels came to have from the third century. Nor is 'the breaking of bread' a communion service in any kind of form we might recognize, beyond the sharing of simple food. Nevertheless, Luke's account in Acts, be it idealistic or historically accurate, suggests attention to practices out of which both the Bible as we know it, and holy communion as we receive it, have grown.

Luke's reference to the apostles' teaching is especially interesting in that it points to the emergence of other sources regarded as authoritative and given attention alongside the scriptures of his day (which certainly included the stories of 'Moses and all the prophets' referred to by the Risen One on the way to Emmaus). How new material like 'the apostles' teaching' came over time to be regarded as scripture is most certainly closely related to its use in the church's worship.

In the book of Revelation, we find letters sent to various churches (Rev. 2–3), and this seems to reflect a practice common in the early church. We know little for sure beyond that letters were read before the early assemblies, though practices from the Jewish tradition – some of which were known in the synagogue of Luke's day – may hint at possible ways in which they were regarded. Synagogue practice was shaped around forms recorded in the Hebrew Bible, notably Nehemiah 8.1–12. In that text, we have a description of the people gathering; of scrolls being read aloud by a person who was perhaps elevated on a platform. In Nehemiah's assembly, prayer precedes reading, and ritual gestures – the lifting of hands, the bowing of heads – surround the reading as reverence towards and response to what is heard. Perhaps most importantly, the text is interpreted: 'they gave the sense, so that the people understood the reading' (Nehemiah 8.8).

It is clear from the New Testament that preaching was practised through-out the early church, with the risen Jesus being remembered as mandating teaching (Matt. 28.19; Mark 16.16). At the origin of this widespread preach-ing is, presumably, Jesus himself remembered as reading the scriptures (notably, Luke 4.16–21), and preaching on many occasions. The Gospels and letters written about him – not least about his preaching – became part of the early communities' supplement to whatever scriptures already were held as authoritative among them. So we find the apostle's letters being read in Pauline circles (1 Thess. 5.27; cf. Col. 4.16), as one example of the practice of sending letters to the churches, to which Revelation witnesses.

As a scattering of other New Testament texts echo Luke's clues about read-ing, so there are possible traces within scripture of the emergence of eucha-ristic practice: at Troas, a community 'met to break bread' on Sundays (Acts 20.7), that first day of the week also being the day of the Emmaus encounter earlier in Luke. As Jesus mandated preaching (especially in association with baptism in the Matthean memory, Matt. 28.19–20), so he is remembered as mandating meals: 'do this' is the imperative recorded by both Luke (22.19) and Paul (1 Cor. 11.24–25) in accounts of what came to be called the last supper. Elsewhere in the Gospels, Jesus is oftentimes remembered as shar-ing meals with others. These meals were of different kinds, both ritual meals – such as the Passover, which may have been the context in which the last supper was celebrated – as well as companionship meals with his immediate circle. There are also 'feasts' with strangers – sometimes great crowds of them, as if embodying prophetic visions of the coming dominion of God (such as in Isa. 25.6–10; compare Matt. 8.11 and Luke 13.28–29). If Jesus meant to recall these prophetic visions in his feeding of crowds, it may be that the contemporary religious authorities of his day missed his intentions. However, they certainly noticed Jesus' more intimate meals, which were most certainly a matter of notoriety, and a slur developed against him for supposedly being 'a glutton and a drunkard, a friend of tax-collectors and sinners' (Matt. 11.19; Luke 7.34).

Emerging Shapes of Christian Worship

The first available fulsome account outside the Bible of an act of Christian worship is that of Justin Martyr, who describes worship in Rome around the year AD 150. Justin wrote to the emperor Antoninus Pius and his purpose was primarily apologetic, commending the life of the community of faith to those outside it. It is not clear to us whether his account is idealized, in order to create the best possible impression; whether it is a description of a 'one-off' event that varied from week to week; or whether it is the embedded and regular pattern of worship for a community. Nor is it clear whether what happened in Rome (or Justin's part of it) was related to what happened in other churches at the time. All this notwithstanding, Justin's record – as the earliest of any we have – is frequently regarded as of great significance for providing insight into the liturgical practice of at least some (the only ones we know about!) early Christians.

In chapter 67 of his first *Apology*, Justin writes:

On the day named after the sun all, whether they live in the city or the countryside, are gathered together in unity. Then the records of the apostles or the writings of the prophets are read for as long as there is time. When the reader has concluded, the presider in a discourse admonishes and invites us into the pattern of these good things. Then we all stand together and offer prayer. And, as we said before, when we have concluded the prayer, bread is set out to eat, together with wine and water. The presider likewise offers up prayer and thanksgiving, as much as he can, and the people sing out their assent saying the amen. There is a distribution of the things over which thanks have been said and each person participates, and these things are sent by the deacons to those who are not present. Those who are prosperous and who desire to do so, give what they wish, according to each one's own choice, and the collection is deposited with the presider. He aids orphans and widows, those who are in want through disease or through another cause, those who are in prison, and foreigners who are sojourning here. In short, the presider is a guardian to all those who are in need . . .[1]

We can note within this text some echoes of what seemed to be suggested in the New Testament. First of all, as in Troas, here the Christians meet on Sunday, the first day of the week. No reason is given for this at this stage, though we know of later writings that consider Sunday as the primary day for worship because the resurrection event was understood to have taken place on that day. It is quite possible that this was already an established understanding in Justin's time.

Second, Justin's text echoes Acts 2's reference to 'the teaching of the apostles'. By the second century, it seems that at least some of this material may have been written down, and Justin has 'records'. There seems also to be the suggestion that these records are used alongside established scripture, alongside 'the writings of the prophets'. (Of course, in Justin's day, there is still no Bible as we know it, so we cannot talk neatly of Old and New Testaments, nor of 'Christian scripture' – even though the idea of Hebrew scripture makes some sense in this context.) Following the readings, the presider presents some kind of sermon, and Justin gives us a clue to its purpose: to invite listeners 'into the pattern of good things'. (An alternative reading is 'into the pattern of beautiful things' – a good image for preachers in any era!)

Third, prayer follows attention to the word. People stand to pray, apparently. (And it is worth noting that although this practice has diminished as a posture for intercession in living memory in Britain, it is still commonplace for gathered prayer throughout much of the world, and has in any case, been normative throughout Christian history.)

Fourth, the assembly includes the table: food is set out, thanks are offered, a meal is shared and portions are sent out to those not present. Finally, a collection takes place for those in need.

The Contemporary Relevance of Justin Martyr

The significance of Justin's record will be immediately apparent to readers who worship in any mainstream denomination, and to those whose participation in liturgy is guided by a recent book of worship in almost any denomination. Celebrations of the eucharist in Roman Catholic, Lutheran, Reformed, Methodist, Baptist and other traditions are often consciously shaped on the description Justin Martyr gives us: people gather, the word is opened and discussed, this moves into prayer, and thanks are voiced around the table. Then there is a sending out. Consider, for instance, the structure for the celebration of mass in the Roman Catholic tradition:

Introductory rites
    Entrance procession
Greeting
    Opening rite –
Rite of blessing
and sprinkling
with water (or)
    Penitential rite (or)
    Litany of praise (or)
    Kyrie (or)
    Gloria (or)
    Other opening rites
    Opening prayer

Liturgy of the word
    Biblical readings
    Responsorial psalm
    Gospel acclamation
    Gospel reading
    Homily
    Profession of faith
    General intercessions

Liturgy of the eucharist
    Preparation of the gifts –
    Preparation of the altar
    Preparation of the gifts –
    Placing of the gifts on the altar
    Mixing of wine and water
    Incense
    Washing of hands
    Prayer over the gifts
    Eucharistic prayer –
    Dialogue
    Preface
    Sanctus acclamation
    Epiclesis
    Institution narrative and
    consecration
    Memorial acclamation
    Anamnesis and offering
    Intercessions
    Doxology
    Communion rite –

The Lord's prayer
    Sign of peace
    Breaking of the bread
Communion –
Private preparation of the priest
Invitation to communion
Distribution of communion
    Communion song
    Cleansing of vessels

Period of silence or song of praise
Prayer after communion

Concluding rite
    Announcements
    Greeting
Blessing
Dismissal[2]

Or, as a Protestant example, take the order for holy communion in the British *Methodist Worship Book*:

THE GATHERING OF THE PEOPLE OF GOD
The presiding minister and the people gather in God's name.
Notices may be given and news items may be shared.

Acts of approach and praise are offered in song and prayer.
A prayer of penitence is followed by an assurance of God's forgiveness.

There may be a brief introduction to the service.
A short prayer reflecting the season or festival is offered.

THE MINISTRY OF THE WORD
The scriptures are read, concluding with a passage from the Gospels.
God's word is proclaimed and shared in songs, hymns, music, dance and other art forms, in a sermon, or in comment, discussion and in silence.

Prayers are offered for the church, for the world and for those in need; a remembrance is made of those who have died; and the Lord's prayer may be said.

THE LORD'S SUPPER
The Peace is introduced by an appropriate sentence of scripture and may be shared by the presiding minister and the people.

The offerings of the people may be placed on the Lord's table.

The presiding minister takes the bread and wine and prepares them for use.

The presiding minister leads the great prayer of thanksgiving:
The people are invited to offer praise to God.
There is thanksgiving
For creation
For God's self-revelation
For the salvation of the world
through Christ
and for the gifts of the Holy Spirit
with special reference to the season or festival.
God's glory may be proclaimed in a version of 'Holy, holy, holy'.
The story of the institution of the Lord's supper is told.
Christ's death and resurrection are recalled.
God is asked to receive the worshippers' sacrifice of praise.
There is prayer for the coming of the Holy Spirit
that the gifts of bread and wine may be, for those who are participating, the body and blood of Christ.

The worshippers, offering themselves in service to God, ask to be united in communion with all God's people on earth and in heaven.

The prayer concludes with all honour and glory being given to God, the Father, the Son and the Holy Spirit, the people responding with a loud 'Amen'.

The Lord's prayer is said, if it has not been said earlier.

The presiding minister breaks the bread in silence, or saying an appropriate sentence.

The presiding minister and people receive communion, after which the elements that remain are covered.

PRAYERS AND DISMISSAL
A short prayer is offered in which the worshippers thank God for the communion and look forward to the final feast in God's kingdom.

There may be a time of praise.

The presiding minister says a blessing and sends the people out to live to God's praise and glory.[3]

These extended quotations from contemporary service books owe a great deal to Justin Martyr. It is obvious that both give more detail than is found in Justin (though, especially in the case of the *Sacramentary*, additional details are often also shaped on early records available to us from the century or so after Justin), but their indebtedness to an account of Sunday worship in Rome in AD 150 is nevertheless transparent. The Roman and Methodist traditions are just two of many possible examples, and the encouragement of the very same pattern in the documents of the World Council of Churches (WCC) has meant that this ancient shape has come to influence the orders of churches in much of the Protestant world. What the WCC says about the shape of the eucharist is much more succinct than either of the two examples already cited, and closer to Justin for it. The World Council of Churches affirms that, liturgically, holy communion consists of:

GATHERING of the assembly into the grace, love and *koinonia* [fellowship] of the triune God

WORD-SERVICE
Reading of the scriptures of the Old and New Testaments
Proclaiming Jesus Christ crucified and risen as the ground of our hope
(and confessing and singing our faith)
and so *interceding* for all in need and for unity
(sharing the peace to seal our prayers and prepare for the table)

TABLE-SERVICE
Giving thanks over bread and cup
Eating and drinking the holy gifts of Christ's presence
(collecting for all in need)
and so

BEING SENT (DISMISSAL) in mission in the world.[4]

What can be seen from each of these examples, among many possible others, is that scripture and sacrament together are central to the order, its very heart.

Shared Centrality of Word and Sacrament

Recent emphasis on the shared centrality of scripture and sacrament has meant that both Catholic and Protestant traditions have shifted some of their inherited emphases. In the Roman Catholic tradition, the Second Vatican Council document on the liturgy, *Sacrosanctum concilium*, spoke of a need for 'the treasures of the Bible ... to be opened up more lavishly so that a richer fare may be provided for the faithful at the table of God's word'.[5] This call for fresh appreciation of the Bible was, in many places, a key part of the renewal of Catholic worship, and has borne fruit ecumenically in that it led to the development of a lectionary (a disciplined pattern of biblical reading) called the Lectionary for Mass that later become the basis for the Revised Common Lectionary which is now used widely throughout the Protestant churches (though with slight, but largely insubstantial, variations).

The Revised Common Lectionary (RCL) is incorporated into almost all recent prayer books across the Protestant traditions and is, essentially, an adaptation of the Lectionary for Mass that shares the same pattern of an Old Testament reading, Psalm and Epistle culminating in a Gospel reading for each Sunday of the year. The readings are arranged in a three-yearly cycle, focusing on Matthew, Mark and Luke in turn, and typically concentrating the reading of John on 'golden days' and special days and seasons of the church's year. So the Johannine prologue is read at Christmastime, the Johannine passion narrative on Good Friday, the Johannine resurrection narratives at Easter, and so on.

The wider links between readings and the church year in the Lectionary for Mass were also carried over into the RCL, introducing many Protestants – sometimes for the first time – to the riches of the liturgical calendar. It is now an extraordinary feature of contemporary Christianity that, through the related Lectionary for Mass and RCL, it is possible to worship in a wide range of denominations, in any continent, and find the same scriptures opened up to the assembly on any given Sunday. The lectionary is, therefore, rightly regarded as a remarkable ecumenical achievement.

It should be noted that different traditions expect and require use of this common pattern of readings to different extents. *Worship from the United*

Reformed Church (2003), for instance, suggests that use of the lectionary is 'appropriate', though the preface of the book states that none of it is to be regarded as prescribed. *Worship from the United Reformed Church* is interesting also for continuing to represent some resistance (characteristic of classical Protestant priorities) to some of the lectionary's dynamics. By culminating in a reading from the Gospel – as the *Methodist Worship Book* (1999) and the Church of England's *Common Worship* (2000) expect – the lectionary's hermeneutic is effectively to 'give the last word to Jesus' and use the Gospel as the key interpretive lens on the rest of the Bible. However, in its orders, *Worship from the United Reformed Church* does not always distinguish the Gospel reading from 'New Testament Reading(s)' (e.g. First Order of Holy Communion),[6] and, sometimes, while a rubric suggests 'A reading from a Gospel', this is explicitly qualified by the following words in brackets '(and/or other New Testament book)' (e.g. Second Order of Holy Communion).[7] Clearly, *Worship from the United Reformed Church* sits more loosely to the Gospel culmination of the RCL pattern than either the Anglican or Methodist book.[8]

At the same time, 'following the lectionary' in the Church of England involves considerable freedoms, and these are often not appreciated. Although 'authorized lectionary provision [is] not matter for local decision except where that provision permits',[9] that 'except' permits wide exceptions: *Common Worship* outlines the rule that during the Christmas cycle (from Advent Sunday through to Candlemas) and the Easter cycle (from Ash Wednesday through to Pentecost) and on All Saints Day, the prescribed readings must be used.[10] However, outside those times – all of 'ordinary time' and, therefore, a majority of each year – local lectionaries may be produced 'for pastoral reasons or preaching or teaching purposes'.[11] In the Anglican context, the creation of a local scripture reading scheme requires 'consultation' between the parish church council and minister, but is entirely permissible. Furthermore, *New Patterns for Worship* (2002) suggests some avenues of departure from the 'set' readings, and models the construction of local reading and sermon series. 'Section C' of *New Patterns for Worship* provides numerous forms of 'modular Bible readings'.[12] These tend to focus in on particular books or portions of canonical books, or take thematic approaches to particular subjects. *New Patterns for Worship* suggests that churches constructing local lectionaries 'should ensure that an adequate amount of Scripture is chosen; that justice is done to the balance of the book and to the general teaching of Scripture; that appropriate Gospel passages are included if the services include Holy Communion; and that the PCC or an appropriate lay group is involved in the decisions'.[13] This is sound guidance in any context.

Corresponding to the increased appreciation of scripture in the Catholic tradition, Protestantism has experienced a renewal of interest in the sacraments. In some cases, this has meant a recovery of the emphasis on the sacraments for which the founding figures of movements had hoped and intended. So, for example, in the British Anglican tradition, one expression of the influence of the Liturgical Movement, the twentieth-century 'Parish Communion Movement', saw an increasing number of parishes come to celebrate holy communion on a weekly basis as the central act of Sunday worship. The evangelical stream of English Anglicanism was the last of the various shades of the church to embrace this priority, but evangelical assent to the centrality of the eucharist following their 1967 conference at Keele meant that the eucharist became the primary form of worship across the whole of the Church of England. This, in its own way, brought the church into the ideal of Thomas Cranmer to have the Lord's supper as the central act of worship. However, Cranmer's ideal had never been widely followed at any previous point in the history of the Church of England, and word services such as matins and evensong in fact became, for centuries, the staple of many Anglicans' experience of worship.

The Methodist churches provide another example. Holy communion has, in many Methodist congregations, become a much more frequent – if not always weekly – celebration than was the case even 50 years ago. This increased frequency of celebration more closely mirrors the hopes of the Methodist pioneers, the Wesley brothers John and Charles, whose own eucharistic spirituality is testified in the collection of *Hymns of the Lord's Supper*. The same shift can be seen in the Reformed churches, in which more frequent celebration of the Lord's supper is also becoming common, and which moves those churches closer to the hope of John Calvin that 'no assembly of the church should be held without the Word being preached, prayers being offered, and the Lord's Supper administered, and alms given' (*Institutes* IV.xvii.44).

At the heart of the twentieth-century Liturgical Movement's achievements was a gathering of concern to identify a shared inheritance of what might be considered 'the essentials of Christian worship'.[14] Vatican II gave unprecedented approval and energy to these concerns. The shared inheritance was largely based on historical reconstruction of worship practice in the early centuries, in which Justin Martyr is a key witness.

In considering the concerns that have preoccupied those persons associated with the Liturgical Movement, it is helpful to keep in focus the notion of a liturgical 'canon', as this has been significant to many subsequent commentators. Such a construct is comparable in some ways to the canon of scripture in so far as it is constituted by elements which are considered to be early, authentic and abiding, though of rite rather than biblical text. And as with the scriptural corpus, there are varying views about the precise content of such a canon. In the liturgical case, many traditions tend to look for verification of their practice by sifting records and assumptions of earlier times in ways which justify the construal of their particular patterns of prayer. Nevertheless, quite considerable consensus about the essentials of Christian worship has been achieved, at least among the 'mainstream' or 'old-line' churches.

Included in the liturgical 'canon' according to the Catholic and many (though not all) mainstream Protestant traditions, are the eucharist; those pastoral offices which correlate closely with the sacraments of the Catholic tradition – though with a particular renewed emphasis on initiation; offices of daily prayer; and cycles of time expressed in seasons and feasts. Some of the elements of this liturgical 'canon' have greater or lesser influence in particular traditions, just as different elements are regarded as supreme in certain traditions and not others. For instance, the primacy of the eucharist in the Roman and many other traditions might be regarded as being analogous to the primacy of the Gospel reading in the lectionary chain which provides a context for interpretation of canonical scripture in the custom of many churches: it is an interpretative lens for all the other aspects.

If widespread recognition of a liturgical canon is a major achievement of the Liturgical Movement, another of its fruitful endeavours has been to facilitate, to a very significant extent, the convergence of structures of liturgical rites. Though this affects many aspects of Christian worship, it has, as we have seen, been particularly the case in relation to holy communion regarded as a 'service of word and table' in which the disciplined, lectionary-based reading and proclamation of scripture has a central place.

As structures of rites converged in these ways, the texts of rites have similarly become a focus of ecumenical consensus. Recovery and study of early liturgical texts and rubrics has led to their incorporation into many recent expressions of liturgical creativity. While Justin Martyr leaves us no forms of prayer, other ancient Christian writers do: the most vivid example in relation to the eucharist is the now common use of the *Apostolic Tradition* in the formulation of modern texts for eucharistic prayer.[15] (We explore this text below.)

Finally, alongside the recovery of primary texts of prayer such as Hippolytus, the Liturgical Movement has encouraged and facilitated shared attention to secondary sources. A contemporary example is the 'ecumenical treasure' of *Sacrosanctum concilium* itself, and more recently again the so-called 'Lima Document' which was the 111th paper of the Faith and Order Commission of the World Council of Churches, *Baptism, Eucharist and Ministry*.[16] Such secondary texts have enabled consensus by providing alternative 'authorities' to the texts around which Reformation and Counter-Reformation controversies were centred, be they the documents of the Council of Trent, Luther's *Catechism*, Zwingli's treatise *On the Lord's Supper*, Cranmer's revised liturgies, or whatever.

In noting the increased role of scripture in the Roman Catholic mass, and the more frequent celebration of the sacrament of holy communion in traditionally word-centred Protestant traditions, we get the sense of some remarkable and wholesale change in patterns for worship in the different traditions. It is fair to say that the renewed emphasis on either scripture or sacrament in traditions where – at least in living memory – the emphasis was downplayed, or lost, has not always been appreciated by those within the traditions. Yet, as noted with the lectionary, there has, in some contexts, been some vigorous resistance to some emphases of liturgical change, with Catholics sometimes feeling that they have been 'Protestantized' and Protestants sometimes feeling that they have been 'Catholicized'. No doubt congregational experience of recovering forgotten elements of the tradition is not always good, and we may note that as a result of the Liturgical Movement, while the role of the sermon was certainly enriched in much of the Catholic world, there has probably been a 'diminution of the offices, which in the Book of Common Prayer are services of the Word . . . [and of] sermons in the Church of England [which] have become fewer and shorter'.[17] Making this point, the Methodist liturgist Gordon Wakefield's caution was that, in the midst of renewal, we should beware of 'impoverishment'. At the same time it should be noted that the renewal of scripture in Catholic worship and the renewal of sacrament in Protestant worship measures up as a very significant kind of convergence of once markedly different foci and experiential centres of worship.

Furthermore, it should be noted that these renewals in Catholic and Protestant worship have meant that both have come to better reflect the presence of both word and sacrament in Justin Martyr's second-century witness to the shape of the liturgy. By diverse traditions giving attention to Justin's testimony, there has been, as the liturgical scholar Geoffrey Wainwright highlights, either 'docking of excrescences or . . . the rebuilding of missing parts'.[18] The work of the World Council of Churches in the process around the 'Lima document', *Baptism, Eucharist and Ministry*, has been a crucial factor in establishing a balance between word and sacrament throughout many Christian traditions; so much so that it is now widely agreed that 'Sunday worship, in its fullness, includes both word and table'. Some churches have even opted to call their Sunday service simply 'Word and Table', a clear statement of the hope of recovery of a balance between these two central elements.[19] And one of the collects from the Roman *Sacramentary*, published in the ecumenical collection *Opening Prayers*, beautifully celebrates what has been achieved:

Wise and gracious God,
you spread a table before us
and nourish your people with the word of life
and the bread from heaven.
In our sharing of these holy gifts,
show us our unity in you
and give us a taste of the life to come . . .[20]

A Fourfold Flow

It is also worth noting how the shape of the eucharistic service, derived from Justin, has influenced the order of other (non-eucharistic) patterns of Christian worship. For instance, the *Methodist Worship Book* suggests that its services of the word are shaped around a fourfold pattern of 'Preparation, Ministry of the Word, Response and Dismissal'.[21] Here, the third part of the order – what the World Council of Churches statement calls the 'table-service' – is replaced by 'Response'. It is suggested, however, that this 'response' emphasizes thanksgiving, an obvious parallel to the 'eucharistic prayer'. Similarly, the Church of England's contemporary services – both word-centred and sacramental – are composed with a similar shape in mind: as the preface to *Common Worship* states: 'the journey through the liturgy has a clear structure with signposts for those less familiar with the way. It moves from the gathering of the community through the Liturgy of the Word to an opportunity of transformation, sacramental or non-sacramental, after which those present are sent out to put their faith into practice.'[22] In *God's Pattern*, David Stancliffe develops attractive correlations between the four parts of the eucharistic service and the dynamic notions of engaging (gathering), attending (the word-service), transforming (the table-service), and energizing (sending out).[23] What is more, he uses the fourfold pattern to think creatively about other aspects of worship: writing about its links with the liturgical seasons:

> The gathering or preparation [is] the advent or time of preparation in our worship, when we long for God's coming and tune our ears and eyes to recognize his presence.

> The Liturgy of the Word [is] the Christmas, or celebration of the Word made flesh, coming among us to engage with us . . .

> The Liturgy of the Sacrament [is] God's transforming of our life by taking it into the passion and resurrection of Jesus Christ's dying and rising . . .

> The Dismissal [is] the moment of Pentecost, when the scattered disciples

finally realized that God had given them all they needed to engage in their apostolic mission ...[24]

The fourfold pattern of Christian worship, with word-and-table in the centre, discerned in Justin Martyr and related to the scriptural hints found in Luke, has rich significance for Christian worship in our present time.

Interplay between Word and Sacrament

An exploration of the relationship between word and sacrament might well also take the liturgy document of Vatican II as its starting point. Paragraph 7 of *Sacrosanctum concilium* suggests that divine presence is to be found in the eucharist in the ministry of the presiding priest, in the sacramental matter, in the sacramental action, in the word and in the holy people celebrating:

> Christ is always present in His Church, especially in her liturgical celebra-tions. He is present in the sacrifice of the Mass, not only in the person of His minister, 'the same now offering, through the ministry of priests, who formerly offered himself on the cross', but especially under the eucharistic species. By His power He is present in the sacraments, so that when a man baptizes it is really Christ Himself who baptizes. He is present in His word, since it is He Himself who speaks when the holy scriptures are read in the Church. He is present, lastly, when the Church prays and sings, for He promised: 'Where two or three are gathered together in my name, there am I in the midst of them' (Matt. 18.20).

There are, of course, some traditional Catholic emphases in the statement – notably the sense that Christ is present 'especially under the eucharistic species' – an emphasis that might disappoint some Protestant readers (and which has been lamented by some Catholic commentators). Nevertheless, the 'diffusal' of divine presence suggested in this statement resists oversimple kinds of localization, and is in many respects congenial to Protestant sen-sibilities. It is notable also that, while the statement retains its 'especially' in relation to 'the eucharistic species', the various 'locations' of God's self-giving affirmed in paragraph 7 of *Sacrosanctum concilium* are all the subject of reverence and honour in Roman Catholic liturgical forms: the people, the scriptures, the elements, and the minister are all censed with incense, or receive a profound bow in recognition of their close association with the presence of Christ.[25]

There is a long and rich tradition within Christianity that celebrates the kind of 'diffusion' we find in *Sacrosanctum concilium* 7. For example, the sense that the word is sacramental, not least in the various mysterious scriptural images of the scrolls being eaten: Ezekiel 2.8—3.3 and Revelation 10.10. The Hebrew tradition also includes injunctions to bind the words of the Shema – 'Hear, O Israel: the Lord is our God, the Lord alone. You shall love the Lord your God with all your heart' (Deut. 6.4) – to the body: 'bind them as a sign on your hand, fix them as an emblem on your forehead' (Deut. 6.8). This tradition survives to this day in Orthodox Judaism in the tradition known as 'laying tefilin' in which adult males engage every day – tying a phylactery containing this part of the law – to their arm for prayer in the morning. An analogous tradition carries over into some styles of Christian worship, with the ritual gesture of marking the first word of the Gospel reading at mass with the sign of the cross, and then repeating the sign over the forehead, lips and heart – an embodied prayer that the word would take residence within.[26]

If the word has sacramental dimensions, so the sacraments have been seen as 'visible words'. Augustine wrote: 'Add the word to the element, and there results a sacrament, as if itself also a kind of visible word',[27] and, notably, Calvin cites this saying of Augustine with approval. Following Calvin, many Protestant traditions hold that language remains somehow key to sacramentality, with sacraments being seen as actions intimately linked to the word. In baptism, for example, water is poured as God's name is pronounced over a person: 'I baptize you in the name of the Father, and of the Son, and of the Holy Spirit.' And although now in those Protestant traditions, as elsewhere, the relation of the sacraments to particular Gospel stories is often regarded as very complex, it remains that it has often been common to link the 'Gospel sacraments' of baptism and holy communion to specific injunctions of Jesus remembered in the Gospels: 'Go . . . make disciples . . . baptize them in the name' (Matt. 20.19), 'do this' (Luke 22.19).[28] Notwithstanding the problems of linking the institution of sacraments to particular scriptural texts, what the sacraments can be seen to do is enact a word of scripture, or portray part of its message. The idea that sacramental signs speak has a range of ancient precedents: and one interesting example, which has recently received emphasis in the World Council of Churches' convergence document on baptism is the testimony of the second-century Christian martyr Ignatius of Antioch, who wrote of his impending death: 'There is water living and speaking in me, saying to me from within, "Come to the Father". I do not delight in the food of death nor in the pleasures of this life. I want the bread of God, which is the flesh of Jesus Christ.'[29] Here, water speaks.

Eucharistic Prayer

Contemporary table prayers often share a basic shape based on documents recovered from the life of the early church, typically from a little later than Justin Martyr's broader description of a worship event. The first form of a eucharistic prayer we have available to us is from c. AD 215 and for a long time ascribed to the hand of Hippolytus, and known as the *Apostolic Tradition*.[30] Whereas Justin suggested that in his day in his congregation the presider 'offers up prayer and thanksgiving, as much as he can, and the people sing out their assent saying the amen', the *Apostolic Tradition* leaves us an actual text:

> The Lord be with you.
> And with your spirit.
> Up with your hearts.
> We have (them) with the Lord.
> Let us give thanks to the Lord.
> It is fitting and right.

> We render thanks to you, O God, through your beloved child Jesus Christ, whom in the last times you sent to us a savior and redeemer and angel of your will; who is your inseparable Word, through whom you made all things, and in whom you were well pleased. You sent him from heaven into a virgin's womb; and conceived in the womb, he was made flesh and was manifested as your Son, being born of the Holy Spirit and the Virgin.

Fulfilling your will and gaining for you a holy people, he stretched out his hands when he should suffer, that he might release from suffering those who have believed in you.

And when he was betrayed to voluntary suffering that he might destroy death, and break the bonds of the devil, and tread down hell, and shine upon the righteous, and fix a term, and manifest the resurrection, he took bread and gave thanks to you, saying, 'Take, eat; this is my body, which shall be given for you.' Likewise also the cup, saying, 'This is my blood, which is shed for you; when you do this, you make my remembrance.'

Remembering therefore his death and resurrection, we offer to you the bread and the cup, giving you thanks because you have held us worthy to stand before you and minister to you.

And we ask that you would send your Holy Spirit upon the offering of your holy Church; that, gathering her into one, you would grant to all receive the holy things (to receive) for the fullness of the Holy Spirit for the strengthening of faith in trust; that we may praise and glorify you through your child Jesus Christ; through whom be glory and honor to you, to the Father and the Son, with the Holy Spirit, in your holy Church, both now and to the ages of ages. Amen.[31]

The text is often transposed into prayers found in contemporary prayer-books, and some of its language will make it instantly recognizable to some readers: 'he stretched out his arms in suffering' is a vivid image that has been one of this ancient prayer's attractions.

The indebtedness of countless eucharistic prayers to the *Apostolic Tradition* will be obvious in many ways. The *Apostolic Tradition* suggests that eucharistic prayer begins with a dialogue: 'Lift up your hearts' (*sursum corda*, the Latin, being the name often given to this exchange). It suggests that this opening dialogue is followed by prayer blessing God for God's work. Thus far, the prayer may well be modelled on Jewish practice as contemporaneous Jewish traditions such as the Talmud are characterized by a presider's call, response by all present and then an extended blessing of the divine. The *Apostolic*

Tradition is also redolent with images from the scriptures: Hippolytus' first paragraph relates the central Gospel designations 'Word' and 'Son', stresses the strange conception of Jesus, gives considerable focus to the cross and mentions the resurrection, all before turning attention to 'the last supper'. The *Apostolic Tradition*'s narrative of the Lord's supper ('He took bread') is surrounded by a complex of language about Jesus ('remembering' – the Greek is a rich word, *anamnesis*), the Holy Spirit ('send your Holy Spirit') and the church as a 'holy people' who bring an 'offering'. Each of these features has remained durable – though at times in the history of the church, charged and controversial – aspects of prayer at the table.

While the later tradition of eucharistic prayer added some things to the *Apostolic Tradition*'s example – notably the conflation of the Isaiah vision and triumphal entry (otherwise known as the Sanctus and Benedictus) – other things were lost. The immediate context around this prayer-text gives a number of further clues about the prayer and it is notable that, like Justin Martyr's suggestion that the presider 'offers up prayers and thanksgiving, as much as he can', though providing a text, the *Apostolic Tradition* also seems to allow for extemporization. It explains that the presider might follow his prayer 'not saying [it] word for word, but to similar effect'.[32] Also, the prayer at the table was complemented by thanksgiving for the word; for example, one prayer focusing on scripture praises God for 'making the bitterness of the heart sweet by the gentleness of [God's] word'.[33] Furthermore, some rubrics in the *Apostolic Tradition* suggest the outlines of ritual that 'clothed' the text for prayer: an example of one such ritual which has proved very durable (note that it is included in the components of the Roman Catholic mass listed earlier in this chapter) is the mixing of water and wine at the preparation of the table. These ritual actions have shaped mandatory ceremonial in some traditions (such as the Roman Catholic), while the notes on ritual in the *Apostolic Tradition* have not been appropriated in any official way in other later traditions that are in other ways indebted to it. Intriguingly, it seems from the *Apostolic Tradition* that the sacramental 'matter' in the celebration for which it leaves a text appears to be wider than bread and wine alone: oil, cheese and other 'things' are prayed over and ascribed symbolic significance in these prayers.[34] Finally, the prayer ascribed to Hippolytus is specifically that for the consecration of a bishop – and we simply do not know whether its use was limited to such occasions, or used in more 'general' celebrations of communion. It claims to represent an inherited tradition ('the tradition that has remained until now'),[35] and so it is at least possible that it may provide access to patterns of eucharistic prayer before the third century, but just how and exactly what is opaque.

There are, then, clearly many questions about the *Apostolic Tradition* – at least as many as there are about Justin Martyr. Yet, as with Justin, the importance of the *Apostolic Tradition* for the shape of the eucharist (and for the eucharistic prayer in particular) is inestimable.

The Interplay of Word and Sacrament

The considerable interplay of word and sacrament, present in the *Apostolic Tradition*, is a particularly significant and durable feature of eucharistic prayer. Prayers around the table typically teem with scriptural images, and offer rich recollection of biblical narratives: not only the 'remembrance' of the last supper, but proclamation of God's many and varied mighty acts. The last supper is usually the focus of the central section of the prayer, but classic patterns of eucharistic prayer open by recalling God's work in creation, covenant and the mission of Jesus. This larger scriptural vision provides the context for the narrower focus on Jesus' meal on the night before his death. And from that wider context, various fragments of quotation are collected in the prayer: the first words echo the scriptural acclamation made, among other examples, by the angel Gabriel to Mary: 'the Lord be with you'. The song that often marks out the first and second sections ('Holy, holy, holy') is itself a juxtaposition of two scriptural pericopes: the vision of Isaiah and the song of the crowd as Jesus enters Jerusalem. And, furthermore, it is notable that the movement of the prayer is basically trinitarian – first of all praising the first Person, then focusing on Jesus, and finally inviting the Spirit.

A 'Classical Pattern' of Eucharistic Prayer

A handful of other texts, from the centuries following Hippolytus, do seem to follow the example of the *Apostolic Tradition* in many respects, though including the Sanctus as a pretty consistent feature, and a discernable shape to eucharistic prayer had emerged within a few centuries. It looked something like this:

- *Sursum corda* (Lift up your hearts)
- Preface (praising God for mighty acts in creation and redemption, focusing on Christ Jesus), probably modelled on Jewish blessing prayers
- Sanctus ('Holy, holy, holy!' – though missing from the *Apostolic Tradition*)
- Benedictus ('Blessed is the one who comes in the Lord's name')
- (Sometimes an epiclesis [invocation of the Holy Spirit] upon the people present and/or the bread and wine placed on the table appears at this point as well as later)
- An institution narrative (Jesus' 'do this')
- Anamnesis (a rich and active kind of 'remembrance') of Christ Jesus
- Epiclesis
- Oblation (offering of, variously, the people's praise, lives of service, bread and wine)
- Doxology

This shape can be traced in virtually all contemporary prayers at the table in the prayerbooks of a vast and diverse range of Christian traditions. Notably, it is now common that the whole prayer (rather than just a part of it) is regarded as consecratory.

Here is a contemporary eucharistic prayer, 'Triple Praise' by Gail Ramshaw, in which the classical pattern can be clearly discerned, and which is a particularly fine trinitarian expression of Christian faith:

The Spirit of God be with you all.
And also with you.
Lift up your hearts.

We lift them to God.
Give thanks to our God!
All our thanks, all our praise!

Holy God, holy One, holy Three!

Before all this, you were God.
Outside all we know, you are God.
After all is finished, you will be God.
Archangels sound the trumpets, angels teach us to sing.
Saints pull us into your presence.
And this is our song:
Holy, holy, holy, God,
Our life, our mercy, our might.
Heaven and earth are full of your glory.
Save us, we pray, you beyond all.
Blest is the One who comes in your name.
Save us, we pray, you beyond all.

Holy God, holy One, holy Three!

You beyond the galaxies, you under the oceans,
you inside the leaves, you pouring down rain,
you opening the flowers, you feeding the insects,
you giving us your image, you carrying us through the waters,
you holding us in the night.
Your smile on Sarah and Abraham,
your hand with Moses and Miriam,
your words through Deborah and Isaiah –
you lived as Jesus among us, healing, teaching, dying, rising,
inviting us all to your feast.

In the night in which he was betrayed,
Jesus took bread, and gave thanks;
broke it, and gave it to his disciples, saying:

Take, eat; this is my body, given for you.
Do this for the remembrance of me.
Again, after supper, he took the cup, gave thanks,
and gave it for all to drink, saying:
This cup is the new covenant in my blood,
shed for you and for all people for the forgiveness of sin.
Do this for the remembrance of me.

Holy God, we remember your Son,
his life with the humble,
his death among the wretched,
his resurrection for us all:
your wisdom our guide, your justice our strength,
your grace our path to rebirth.

And so we cry, Mercy: **Mercy!**
And so we cry, Glory: **Glory!**
And so we cry, Blessing: **Blessing!**

Holy God, we beg for your Spirit.

Enliven this bread, awaken this body,
pour us out for each other.
Transfigure our minds, ignite your church,
nourish the life of the earth.
Make us, while many, united;
make us, through broken, whole;
make us, despite death, alive.

And so we cry, Come, Holy Spirit:
Come, Holy Spirit!
And so the church shouts, Come, Holy Spirit:
Come, Holy Spirit!
And so the earth pleads, Come, Holy Spirit:
Come, Holy Spirit!

> You, holy God, holy One, holy Three –
> Our Life, our Mercy, our Might,
> Our Table, our Food, our Server,
> Our Rainbow, our Ark, our Dove,
> Our Sovereign, our Water, our Wine,
> Our Light, our Treasure, our Tree,
> Our Way, our Truth, our Life –
> You, holy God, holy One, holy Three!
>
> Praise now, praise tomorrow, praise forever!
> And so we cry, Amen: **Amen!**[36]

However, the influence of the *Apostolic Tradition* and the classical pattern of eucharistic prayer is not confined to those traditions which choose to write down their prayerforms. Ruth Duck, a contemporary prayerwriter in a Reformed tradition, suggests how this classic shape can inspire extempore prayer in 'free churches':

> Those who prefer a much simpler form of eucharistic prayer would do well, however, to incorporate the time-honored theological themes of thanksgiving, remembrance, institution narrative, offering, invocation of the Spirit and rehearsal of God's reign. These themes can be incorporated into extemporaneous prayer, if the presider thoroughly understands the structure and theology of the eucharistic prayer. I provide the following example as a way to incorporate a fuller theology of Holy Communion in a brief prayer:
> We praise you, loving God, for creating all things,
> for making us in your image,
> and for seeking us when we turn to you.
> We thank you for coming to us in Jesus Christ,
> who was faithful even to death on the cross
> and who lives among us still.
> We share this meal in remembrance of him,
> offering you our lives in praise and thanksgiving.
> Fill us with your Spirit, to make us one in Christ,
> and one in love for you and for all people,

as in word and deed we seek your reign of peace and justice on earth.
Glory be to you, eternal God, through Jesus Christ,
in the power of the Holy Spirit. Amen.

The story of the Last Supper would be told in narrative form outside the
prayer. Congregations can learn to say 'Amen' after the closing doxology
and a few seconds of silence . . .[37]

Notably, one key feature of many prayers in the Reformed tradition, seen
in this quotation from Ruth Duck, has been to entirely separate out the
'institution narrative' from the 'classical' prayer (the narrative, because so
obviously scriptural, being regarded as the most important) and to use it as
a 'biblical warrant' – read for edification – before prayer at the table, rather
than incorporated into the prayer. This distinctive feature of Reformed
churches is, however, receding, and it is increasingly common for Reformed churches to provide forms that incorporate the story of the last supper
into the prayer itself, where the *Apostolic Tradition* places it. A recent example
in the British context is *Worship from the United Reformed Church*, whose first
prayer in the communion orders consciously follows the classical shape.

Eucharist and Controversy

As suggested above, some aspects of eucharistic prayer have controversial
histories. Controversy usually revolves around questions of focus: Onto
what is the Spirit invoked? What in particular about Christ is 'remembered'
in the anamnesis? What is 'offered' in the oblation? In very general terms,
the Reformers typically resisted the invocation of the Spirit onto bread and
wine, as in Catholic tradition, but rather invited the Spirit's outpouring upon
the people; the Reformers typically concentrated the anamnesis of Christ,
especially on the cross (as in the stress in the Book of Common Prayer [1662]
on Christ's 'one, full, perfect and sufficient sacrifice once offered for the sins
of the whole world'); and the Reformers typically would countenance the
'oblation' only of 'thanks and praise', counteracting the Catholic sense of
'offering' the sacrament and what it signifies.

Contemporary controversy around the eucharist is less likely to cen-tre on the kinds of issues just noted. Rather, it tends to emerge around the relative significance of a range of biblical material. Most traditions have drawn their understanding of communion especially from the Corinthian correspondence, in which Paul relates an 'institution narrative' for the eucha-rist and goes on to warn against inappropriate participation (1 Cor. 11.23–34). Concern about 'worthy reception' grows out of attention to this and related texts. However, a current trend in biblical scholarship is to expand the range of biblical material understood to be a basis for holy communion. Alongside the Corinthian fragments, some other material, to which we have alluded in this chapter, may also be regarded as of variable significance: Jesus' table-companionship with tax collectors and sinners, his proclamation of the dominion of God as a great banquet, and various miraculous feedings. Scholarship is divided as to how these various emphases ought to influence contemporary understanding of the eucharist,[38] and something of the argu-ment can be seen by cross-referencing, for example, Bruce Chilton's explana-tion of the 'last supper'[39] with a more traditional approach as represented by someone like Tom Wright.[40]

The following short extract from Chilton opens up at least part of what might be at stake in these disagreements, for in Chilton's view, the last supper is not so much a 'forward-looking' commentary on the cross (from 'the night before he died' as eucharistic prayers often stress) as a part of Jesus' argument with the religious authorities in charge of the temple, whose views of purity were so different from his own:

> Jesus claimed that wine and bread were a better sacrifice than what was offered in the Temple, a foretaste of new wine in the kingdom of God. At least wine and bread were Israel's own, not tokens of priestly dominance. No wonder the opposition to him, even among the Twelve (in the shape of Judas, according to the Gospels) became deadly. In essence, Jesus made his meals into a rival altar, and that scandalized many of his followers (see John 6.66–71).[41]

Conclusion

In this chapter, we have surveyed a range of issues related to understanding scripture and sacrament, word and table, as the heart of Christian worship, the things into which Christian worship invites participation. Again and again, we have seen that the two are consistently interrelated, in scripture, in the Christian tradition and in sacramental celebration itself. It is perhaps their interrelationship that has made scripture and sacrament so durable and such strong 'bones' of the liturgy. And it is to the matters which 'enflesh' these bones to which we now turn.

Further Reading

Thomas F. Best and Dagmar Heller (eds), *Eucharistic Worship in Ecumenical Contexts: The Lima Liturgy – and Beyond* (Geneva: WCC Publications, 1995).

Paul Bradshaw, *Eucharistic Origins* (London: SPCK, 2003).

Edward Foley, *From Age to Age: How Christians have Celebrated the Eucharist* (Chicago, IL: Liturgy Training Publications, 1991).

David R. Holeton (ed.), *Our Thanks and Praise: The Eucharist in Anglicanism Today* (Toronto, Ont.: Anglican Book Centre, 1998).

R. C. D. Jasper and G. J. Cuming (eds), *Prayers of the Eucharist: Early and Reformed* (Collegeville, MN: Liturgical Press, 1987).

Gordon Lathrop, *Holy Things: A Liturgical Theology* (Minneapolis, MN: Fortress Press, 1993).

Gail Ramshaw, *Treasures Old and New: Images in the Lectionary* (Minneapolis, MN: Fortress Press, 2002).

Frank Senn, *Christian Liturgy: Catholic and Evangelical* (Minneapolis, MN: Fortress Press, 1997).

Elizabeth Smith, *Bearing Fruit in Due Season: Feminist Hermeneutics and the Bible in Worship* (Collegeville, MN: Liturgical Press, 1999).

Geoffrey Wainwright, *Worship with One Accord: Where Liturgy and Ecumenism Embrace* (New York: Oxford University Press, 1997).

2
Space and Symbol

What is the impact of the architectural and spatial environment on liturgy?
How do symbols speak?
What kinds of ceremony are present in free church traditions of worship?
What visual theology might be communicated by worship space?
How might scripture and symbol amplify each other?

To continue the anatomical analogy with which we began and ended the last chapter, although scripture and sacrament may be the 'bones' of Christian worship, when they are enfleshed they can create very different sizes and shapes. We explore some of the potential for difference in this chapter, thinking about the space in which worship happens when the church gathers, and the symbols employed in their worship activities. Sacrament and scripture at the heart of Christian worship may be celebrated with either more or less elaborate ceremonial, and in buildings of very different kinds – from classical basilicas, to simple meeting houses, to primarily other-purpose buildings like school gymnasiums or sports centres. The architectural and spatial arrangements of these different kinds of spaces strongly influence how non-textual dimensions of liturgy are embodied, what kinds of ceremonial are possible and appropriate and, fundamentally, the extent to and means by which people may participate. Different kinds of spaces – and the ceremonial used within them – communicate a visual theology.

Visual Theologies

Perhaps the key point to be made about space and symbol is that neither are neutral: each communicates profoundly, albeit non-verbally: 'what the eye sees is no less important in conveying theology and calling forth praise than what the ear hears'.[1] Space and symbol actively contribute to the meaning of liturgy, conveying theology that is either a good or poor reflection of what might be preached, professed and enacted within and beyond the building.

Recognition of the formative power of space and symbol is part of understanding liturgy not just as texts, but as something much broader. The context of common prayer, including the physical architectural space in which prayer takes places, and use or non-use of particular ritual patterns and gestures, all actively require conscious reflection and engagement by both students of liturgy and presiders in it, the latter of whom have to learn to manage environment and ambience to best possible effect.

Reading Buildings

Many buildings constructed for Christian worship are ordered in a particular symbol-laden way, and the particular kinds of furniture they house are significant. Consider those church buildings in which the baptismal font is situated close to the main entrance, a physical space that is meant to communicate that baptism is the key means of 'welcome' into the church. At the opposite end of the building, there is an altar table. This may well be situated in its own clearly demarcated space, often separated by either steps or some kind of rail, if not both. Perhaps the altar table is central to a especially richly symbolic area in which majestic images of Christ, the saints and 'the company of heaven' are depicted. In spaces arranged in this kind of way the very positioning of the font and altar table may be intended to 'tell a story', to communicate that the Christian faith is itself a kind of journey – beginning with baptism and culminating in the heavenly feast at which Christ presides. And the 'journey' involved in movement front font to altar table may also be underlined – or overshadowed – by another key architectural feature: a vaulting roof that recalls the hull of a boat, or an ark, for safe travel between birth into the world and presence among the multitudes of heaven.

Church buildings that 'speak' in the way suggested are easy to find in Britain and much of Europe. Of course, not all church buildings tell the same story, and buildings that speak somewhat differently are also not hard to find. In some the central feature is, rather than a table, a pulpit or place of preaching, which may, literally, tower over a congregation (and communion table) as a way of 'saying' something about the priority of God's word in the congregation's understanding of God's gracious gifts. A significant number of free church buildings are arranged more or less like this, with the pulpit as the central feature.

Even then, there are some very interesting further possibilities. Quaker meeting houses are typically arranged on the level, so that no one sits in a higher seat than any one else – reflecting the characteristic Quaker conviction that a separate order of ministers is not required for the proper conduct of Christian worship. Making the same point, the meeting is likely to face inwards, with people sitting around the 'sides' of a simple room, rather than all facing one way towards which there is a particular focus of attention, be it altar table or place for the preaching of the word, or authorized minister. Again, Baptist churches may be organized around a particular central feature – a large baptismal pool – though this is, somewhat strangely, often hidden away under floorboards, at least on many occasions, being opened up from time to time to celebrate the dramatic baptismal events that characterize the Baptist tradition.

The stories these different spaces tell are powerful ones. Each one might offer 'new co-ordinates' for those who participate in the liturgies within them, as David Brown and Ann Loades suggest with respect to the first example above. The buildings offer ways of seeing the life of faith:

The traditional position of the baptismal font at the entrance warns that one is entering a temporal zone which tells a different story from that which begins at one's birth. Then the fact that one has to move through the church to reach the altar speaks of a time which culminates in something other than one's own death, with the promise of sharing Christ's resurrection through participation in his death. The sacred space is thus being used to initiate one into a new time.[2]

Comparing Cathedrals

In the 1960s, Basil Spence created the Anglican cathedral in Coventry,[3] which is perhaps the most well-known example of a new building with a long central axis, within which there is a baptismal font by the entrance which progresses into space oriented towards a 'high altar'. Although the cathedral features a number of pieces of excellent modern art, one in particular – a gigantic tapestry of 'Christ in Glory' by Graham Sutherland – covers the entire eastern wall and provides a very strong visual focus throughout the whole cavernous interior. By contrast, another later twentieth-century English cathedral, Frederick Gibberd's Roman Catholic cathedral in Liverpool, is designed very differently indeed. In that space, the altar table is architecturally central, the congregation sits in concentric circles around it, and the outside edge of the round building leads into seven small chapels, each one associated with a particular sacrament of the Catholic tradition. Above the central altar, the ceiling gathers into a dramatic cylinder of light. The building is a good example of a style of architecture which has retained a strong liturgical focus, but that is organized centrifugally rather than longitudinally, and in which the back row of seats is never far from the main place of liturgical action. This imaginative building in Liverpool is suggestive of a number of recent shifts in thinking about the design of church buildings. In the past half-century, and allied to the influence of liturgical renewal, some new priorities have emerged about constructing and renovating church buildings.

Font, Lectern, Table (and Chair)

In newly built spaces for Christian worship and in renovations of older buildings, there has been much recent emphasis on bringing the whole gathering of worshippers closer to the main areas where liturgical action takes place, hence attempting to better enable their participation. This has often meant that the traditional longitudinal arrangement of space is less popular than it once was. Of course, placing furniture centrally is more straightforward in new buildings, which are much less likely than in previous generations to be longitudinal. As older longitudinal buildings have been renovated, moving key pieces of liturgical furniture has often proved much more difficult to do in ways that are aesthetically pleasing. It has often meant moving the altar table out of the east end and into a south or north side of a large nave space, and rearranging the congregational seating perhaps by turning the assembly to face north or south.

In all traditions, there has been recent thinking about what constitutes the central pieces of liturgical furniture. Reflecting the consensus discussed in the previous chapter, it is now widely agreed that the central pieces of liturgical furniture are those for use with scripture and sacrament, and so alongside an altar table there is now likely to be a prominent lectern, pulpit or place for the word. Situating an altar table and place of the word in close proximity is a significant way of suggesting their related work and equal weight, and in spaces where either one or the other had – perhaps for centuries – dominated, while another was diminutive, reordering the places of word and sacrament in relation to each other conveys a very strong message, a visual theology.

Oftentimes, rather than containing both lectern for reading scripture and pulpit for preaching, there is now just one place for both Bible reading and preaching – and reflecting the sense that 'the treasures of the Bible are to be opened up more lavishly so that the faithful receive richer fare at the table of God's word', the one item for both reading and preaching is itself intended to communicate something about a fresh evaluation of the importance of biblical preaching. In longitudinal spaces, where seating is flexible (or is made flexible by removing and replacing fixed pews with chairs or movable pews) one option has been to place the altar table and lectern at opposite ends of the east–west axis, and to seat the congregation in long rows along the north and south walls, allowing for an emphatic dual focus on scripture and sacrament. This is particularly attractive when a place for baptism can also be accommodated on the axis, perhaps at the mid-point between the altar table and lectern, and hence between the rows of people facing one another with the symbol of their baptism in their sight and at the centre of the gathered community. This, too, is a strong visual theology.

Another increasingly common way of enlarging the emphasis on baptism has been to introduce more generous and dramatic fonts, perhaps immersion pools in Baptist style – though not now so often hidden away under floorboards – but made strong visual features. Introducing flowing water also allows sounds related to baptism to resonate around the building, even when building a larger pool is impossible.[4]

In contemporary reorderings, dual east–west axes are sometimes preferred to circular designs, as centrifugal arrangements have sometimes been critiqued as being overly insular, literally inward-looking. The danger of such a visual theology then becomes that the worshipping community loses focus on its mission in the community, which its circular seating might be seen to exclude. In response, *broken* circles may be regarded as effectively resisting this potential weakness, suggesting the possibility of others being able to find a place, to join the circle because it is never complete. However seating is arranged, in either new or reordered church buildings, a recent concern has been to emphasize the importance of the assembly itself – by drawing it close to the centre of activity, and so aiding participation – while also expressing a spacious openness. At their best, both renovations and new-builds of liturgical space express the dual priorities identified in the American Catholic bishops' document, *Environment and Art in Catholic Worship*: 'a climate of hospitality' that 'invites contemplation'.[5]

Within the context of discussions about seating for the assembly, some differences of opinion should be noted about a chair for the presider. While all of the different Christian traditions agree that three pieces of liturgical furniture are essential – font, lectern and table – the Catholic tradition has tended to regard the presider's chair as a fourth piece of essential furniture. In Catholic liturgical documents, there are suggestions that this chair ought to be placed prominently before the rest of the congregation, so that the presider is clearly visible, and their particular role is evident. Other traditions, sometimes in order to visualize a sense of 'every member ministry', or to show that the ordained's service finds its context in the work of all God's people, have tended to place the presider *among* the congregation. Sometimes, they may not have distinguished a presider's chair, or otherwise may have included a slightly modified seat for the presider among the circle of other seats.

Whether three or four pieces of furniture are regarded as essential, there is general agreement that these pieces of furniture ought to be emphasized within the space for worship, not competing with other pieces of furniture (which often serve no or little purpose), nor lost amid accumulated 'clutter'. This can be complicated, especially in older buildings where some additional pieces of furniture are fixed – like tombs, for instance! – but unnecessary tables, unused chairs, derelict bookcases, idle music stands and manifold other pieces of clutter are easier to remove. Clarifying the main pieces of furniture and clearing space at the main centres of liturgical activity, which lectern, font, table and perhaps chair signify, has been a major task of liturgical renewal in the light of emerging consensus about the dual centrality of scripture and sacrament.

Philadelphia Cathedral, recently reordered under its dean, Richard Giles, an Anglican expert in liturgical architecture and author of *Re-Pitching the Tent*,[6] 'unclutters' the building of generations of accretions and reshapes it as a spacious basilica. The central feature of the apse is the cathedra, the bishop's chair, as in the first Christian use of basilicas. However, in Philadelphia the cathedra is designed as an integral part of a stone bench which extends right around the edge of the building, clearly locating the bishop's ministry among that of the whole worshipping assembly. The building is an embodiment of contemporary liturgical renewal, and is itself explained in another of Richard Giles' books, *Creating Uncommon Worship*.[7]

Clarifying Liturgical Space

How space permits, directs or restricts movement, how pieces of furniture are positioned in relation to one another, and who may use them freely communicates a great deal of importance about the nature of the Christian community and the range of its self-understanding. Environment is an aspect of worship that is simply too important to neglect: in the Methodist James White's pithy phrase: 'space is faith', exciting or inhibiting various understandings of relationship between elements of the faith (like word, baptism and communion) and their relationship with life. Indeed, James White asserts that space is 'perhaps the most important single factor' in worshippers' formation in faith. What White goes on to add is crucial: 'not only does space form faith, it can and frequently does deform and distort faith. Thus we are frequently caught in a conflict between the faith we profess and the faith the building proclaims.'[8] For instance, he draws attention to potential ways in which the architectural environment in which worship is set can deeply agitate participants by giving signals that jar with those that the rites for prayer celebrated in such spaces seek to express. At worst, in White's eyes, the liturgical environment may undermine the possibility of a faith community embodying the grace available in sacramental rites. Hence the work of liturgical renewal to reorder church buildings in ways that allow the central pieces of furniture to 'speak' uncontested, clarified among non-essential furniture and by other visual foci.

The creation or commissioning of interesting, attractive and beautiful vessels and furniture for the central things is another aspect: harmonizing secondary symbols such as fire and light, oil, and so on, in a way which does not detract from the central things is also important; otherwise, they may overshadow the central things most closely associated with scripture and sacrament.

Questions about space often become particularly pressing when worship space is used at other times for other kinds of activities on church premises, and the hospitality of the church in its use of its buildings is often a critical factor in mission to the local community. In spaces used in mission beyond worship, there is, in some places, an interesting trend towards the building of hearths in church buildings that hope to accent hospitality (the idea comes from *Environment and Art in Catholic Worship*). One of the challenges for mission in buildings in which the same space is to be shared for both worship and other community uses is how to help the space – while being accessible – to suggest means of grace.

The message of a space may have much more impact on the congregations who use it than preaching – or other activities – that take place within it. And, importantly, when space is reconfigured, the unspoken 'story' of the space changes. Liturgical renewal of church buildings has encouraged the conscious development of space in relation to the story the Christian community wishes to proclaim.

Space has a visual theology, and decisions about the arrangement of space for worship may even define the range of experience possible within it. For example, the arrangement of either ranked or facing seating may embed particular theologies. Arrangement of the community's seating and the seating's relationship to other pieces of furniture may suggest where divine presence is located – among us or between us may be the interpretation of circular arrangements. Or, conversely, it may suggest that divine presence is beyond us, apart from us, in the case of ranked seating separate from a distinct 'sanctuary', to which only some members of the community have access?

Addressing such questions about the visual theology of space for worship impinges upon thinking about 'the priesthood of all believers', among other things, in that whether the assembled church is able to see one another's faces is likely to have a profound influence on how ministry is personified. Perhaps those in ranked pews, looking only at the back of others' heads, and with sight of only the faces of the ordained are likely to struggle more with a sense of a diversity of ministries among the Christian people.

Other important questions relate to what space is accessible to children in worship. Whether or not children can be visibly approximated to the holy table is more likely than any theological discussion to influence thinking about the appropriateness of children's full sacramental participation. Their visible proximity to the central things of Christian worship may either foster or frustrate the wider church's willingness to welcome them.

A Detailed Example: Portsmouth Cathedral

One of the most exciting recent reordering projects in Britain has been the Cathedral Church of St Thomas of Canterbury in Portsmouth. Parts of the building date from the twelfth century, and it has had a varied history, involving numerous architectural changes and additions. Its recent reordering began in the 1980s under the then dean David Stancliffe, who reconceived the space with the liturgy of the Easter Vigil especially in mind.

The cathedral is now quite deliberately arranged as a series of related, but distinct spaces. The largest of these, the nave, at the west end, is a mid-twentieth-century architectural addition to the older original building which now forms the east end. The nave is a large rectangular area which is surrounded by a raised walkway, rather like an internal cloister, and the walkway is integral to the ambience of the reordered building as a whole, which is designed to facilitate *movement*. It intends to 'communicate a sense of journeying into faith'.[9]

The whole nave space is capable of seating several hundred people, although none of the seating is fixed – there are no pews, and it may be completely emptied of chairs in order to create a very spacious area for multipurpose use. It is meant to have the feel of a 'marketplace' rather than a 'narrowly ecclesial' one.[10] Nevertheless, its main purpose was conceived to be the celebration of Easter, and the nave is the area in which on Holy Saturday night the new fire, from which the paschal candle is lit, provides a dramatic centre. Around the fire, the long scripture readings recounting salvation history are read among the assembly and candidates for baptism may make their vows to renounce evil and turn to Christ.

The Easter vigil then moves to the second of the distinct spaces that houses a large font, and provides a liminal area, a passage, between western nave and east end. Significantly, the font itself is spatially central to the whole building. This space is distinctly enclosed by comparison to the spacious nave. The baptistery is situated under the low ceiling of the central tower, and nearby walls flank the font on north and south. Space is, then, dramatically restricted around the baptistery, and there is a deliberate sense of having to pass through, or close by, the water.

The font is in fact a sizable pool, deliberately inclusive, able to hold an adult or a child, although deliberately tomb-shaped and cruciform in order to recall scriptural imagery, such as that of Romans 6, about believers being baptized into Christ's death and resurrection. It is also eight-sided, and inscribed with a text from a sermon (*Mystagogical Catechesis* 2.4) of the fourth-century bishop of Jerusalem, Cyril, which expands the pool's allusions to death and new life:

> When you went down into the waters it was like night and you could see nothing: but when you came up again, it was like finding yourself in the day. The one moment was your death and your birth; that saving water was both your grave and your mother.

The baptistery admits and welcomes worshippers to the east end of the cathedral, in which the building opens up into a choir area, like the nave, but unlike the baptistery, notably light and roomy. And unlike the nave, this space could by no means be interpreted as a 'marketplace', for it focuses around the central pieces of furniture it houses, lectern and altar table. Proceeding from the font, the area immediately centres on a prominent and noble lectern in the choir, marking this space as especially hospitable to services of the word. At the eastern end of the choir, the large, central altar table is flanked by pulpit to one side and cathedra to the other. The altar is the third piece of furniture sharing the same central axis as pool and lectern, and is situated under the crossing of the original twelfth-century structure.

Beyond the altar table, sheltered by the oldest part of the building, is an antechapel, dedicated to the saint, Thomas, whose name is given to the cathedral. This space is entirely unencumbered by ancillary furniture and a second, smaller, altar table stands dignified by the space that surrounds it. Above this altar table, a pyx holds bread and wine consecrated in celebration of the eucharist and symbolizes the presence of Christ in the midst. The pyx, in the open space of the antechapel, behind the central altar table, and which one approaches in the movement through the building, is intended to provide 'a sign that God is both with, and yet not contained by, his Church'.[11]

Embodying Theology

Another dimension of liturgy that also conveys a visual theology is that of ceremony and gesture. Christian worship styles range from the richly elaborate to the relatively simple. All, however, involve ritual and symbol, even the most vehemently 'non-liturgical' (a term I have argued in the Introduction, is a misnomer). Symbol and ceremony are by no means confined to only certain styles – 'high', 'Catholic' or whatever. It is, however, certainly the case that some traditions have been more ready than others to embrace ritual dimensions of worship. For instance, the liturgy document of the Second Vatican Council suggested that 'to promote active participation, the people should be encouraged to take part by means of . . . actions, gestures and bodily attitudes' (*Sacrosanctum concilium* 30). It is strange, though, that many kinds of Christians have become used to thinking of others as 'ritualists', as opposed to themselves. For some, ritual is strongly opposed to 'word', with God's word at least being valued as more certain, less ambiguous than symbols, signs or body language. For sure, as Bruce Morrill notes, 'to attend to the body in all its multivalency in the Church's liturgy is to attend to the persistently ambiguous condition of our humanity'.[12] And for Christians who live with suspicion of this multivalency, they may need considerable help in coming to recognize the ritual character of their own worshipping styles. However, many suggestive studies are at hand to enable such awareness. For example, Diane Karay Tripp's exploration of daily prayer in the Reformed tradition identifies kneeling, raised hands, beating the breast and prostration as all playing a part in the history of Reformed prayer. In the words of Richard Baxter, 'both words and gestures are the due expression of [the] heart'.[13] Tripp's point is that contemporary Reformed Christians who eschew conscious ritual forms may in fact be neglecting elements of their own tradition. In fact, every style of Christian worship has its rituals, even when they are neglected, forgotten or downplayed.

Likewise, Daniel Albrecht's *Rites in the Spirit*[14] shows how Pentecostal Christians, many of whom might not initially think of themselves as engaged in ritual, are in fact habitually immersed in ceremonial practices. For example, Pentecostal 'altar calls' to step forward and share in fervent prayer ministry or the laying on of hands, or to commit oneself to 'renewed life consecration', often have deeply embedded patterns, and furthermore, may be associated with a particular ritual space – usually that around the altar rail, if present, or else in the open space between the communion table and the first row of chairs or pew. Entering into that space is a ritual gesture, involving particular gestures and ceremonial acts. One of the fascinating points that Albrecht makes is that, in Pentecostal parlance, 'the altars' (in the plural) refers not to a table, or tables, but to this open physical space at 'the front' between table and pew into which people move to participate in the defining modes of Pentecostal worship. (A secondary meaning of 'altar' is in fact the entire movement of response to God, of spiritual sacrifice, in the range of ways that are engaged at 'the front'.)[15]

In traditions that especially treasure preaching, sermons may have highly ritualized elements, although many participants may at first see word and ritual as somewhat opposed to each other. The womanist theologian Dolores

Williams notes some strong ritualized dimensions to preaching in the context of the African-American Baptist tradition in which she was nurtured:

> a certain scenario was acted there nearly every Sunday morning during worship. The minister, who had a deep and loud and resonant voice, began the service by belting out from the pulpit this question to the congregation: 'Who do you say God is?' The huge choir in back of him would respond in song: 'God of Gods, King of Kings, Father everlasting!' The preacher would belt out the same question again: 'Who do you say God is?' Then Sister Sadie Davis, a domestic worker, would come up front from among the congregation and would sing these words in response to the question: 'Poor little Mary's boy, and they nailed him to a tree, and they nailed him to a tree.' The preacher would ask the question again: 'Who do you say God is?' The choir responded: 'God of Gods, King of Kings, Father everlasting!' The preacher asked again: 'Who do you say God is?' Sister Davis responded, 'Poor little Mary's boy, and she laid him in the grave, and she laid him in the grave.' The preacher asked again: 'Who do you say God is?' The choir sang again: 'God of Gods, King of Kings, Father everlasting!' Raising his voice to drumlike proportions, the preacher rolled out the question: 'I say, who do *you* say God is?' Sister Davis's beautiful contralto voice almost screamed the answer: 'Poor little Mary's boy, and he got up from the dead, *and he got up from the dead!*' The preacher would say, 'Well, all right!' Of course, by that time the atmosphere in the church would be electric, and several women would be shouting. Many of the women had sons and daughters and close relatives who were trying to get up from the death of despair, depression, and defeat.[16]

What is so powerful about Williams' testimony is her point as the quotation closes, underlining how the ritual of the sermon engaged the life-experience of those participating.

In these various ways, we can see some embodied aspects of worship. And as these examples suggest, it is also possible that 'bodily signs carry theological convictions at a deeper cultural level than do rationally expressed "beliefs".[17] Don Saliers makes this point to explain how 'conservative Protestants may have more trouble with the use of the sign of the cross or genuflection than with more explicitly doctrinal differences with Roman Catholics',[18] and to explore the point further, we shall unpack one of the examples he cites.

The Language of Signs

Signs and symbols play a very powerful role in worship. Saliers point that some gestures tend to be associated with particular traditions is both obvious and complex: either use or non-use of certain gestures seems often to be a means of defining oneself as part of, or distinct from, a particular tradition. One of the most ancient signs of Christian worship, the sign of the cross, may be considered by some Protestants to be part of Catholic tradition, and hence perhaps avoided within their particular Protestant liturgical style. Similarly, some Christians may regard the raising of hands as a specifically 'charismatic' practice, and so be somewhat hesitant of embracing it. However, neither of these gestures is simply reducible to association with any one tradition or another. In fact, in the early church, it seems that the two different gestures were linked, as in this example from the late first or second century *Odes of Solomon*:

> I extended my hands and hallowed my Lord,
>   for the expression of my hands is his sign.
>   And my extension is the upright cross.
>   Hallelujah.[19]

The *orans* posture (standing with hands stretched out, palms upwards) is depicted in the first-known examples of Christian art, such as those found in the third-century wall paintings in the catacombs around Rome where early Roman Christians were buried. However, a number of early Christian writers who reflect on the posture do not see it simply as an embodiment of scriptural injunctions to 'lift up holy hands' (e.g. 1 Tim. 2.8) in thanksgiving. Typically, they give it a further meaning, understood as refracted through the cross. Standing *orans* – with arms open as if pinned down, or up – identifies the person praying with Christ and gestures the self as a sacrifice.

The origins of the sign of the cross probably lie in this older practice of standing *orans*, though by the late second century, Tertullian wrote of tracing the sign over the body in accompaniment of many everyday activities: 'At every step, when going in and out, when putting on clothes and shoes, when washing ourselves, when kindling the lights, when going to sleep, sitting down, and in every action we place the sign of the cross on our foreheads.'[20] It clearly was not confined to times of public worship.

Although the gesture was jettisoned by some Reformation traditions, others that continued Catholic practices still used the gesture in their liturgies, largely on account of its strong patristic heritage. The Lutheran tradition is an obvious case in point, and one famous twentieth-century advocate of the gesture outside the liturgy, amid the ordinary everyday things of life was Dietrich Bonhoeffer, who suggested use of the sign in his rule for a Christian community, *Life Together*. The rejection of the sign by some at the Reformation was probably due to its growing association with a sacramental formula that Reformers wished to explicitly reject (rather than, say, its association since the time of the Arian controversy with proclamation of orthodox doctrine against heterodoxy), although the sign of the cross was retained in the baptismal services of several Protestant traditions as one of notably few gestures they mandated. In fact, use of the sign in the baptismal context often remains a strong feature of Protestant worship practices and, indeed, it is being recovered in other traditions that were perhaps once unfamiliar with it, now recognizing its ecumenical heritage. Here is an example of use of the sign from the Uniting Church of Australia, comprised of former Methodists and Presbyterians:

An elder pours water into the font.
The elder then says:
Come, Lord Jesus,
refresh the lives of all your faithful people.

The minister says one or more of the following; and may sprinkle water from the font by hand three times towards the people:
Always remember that you are baptized,
and be thankful.
and/or

Always remember that you are baptized,
and give thanks to the risen Lord.
and/or
Always remember that you are baptized,
and praise the Holy Spirit.

The minister may then say:
Today we remember that, from the time of our baptism,
the sign of the cross has been upon us.
I invite you now to join me
in tracing the sign of the cross upon your forehead,
saying – I belong to Christ. Amen.

The minister and the people may mark themselves with the sign, saying:
I belong to Christ. Amen.

The minister may also add:
You may trace the sign of the cross
on those around you,
saying – You belong to Christ. Amen.

The people may mark others with the sign, saying:
You belong to Christ. Amen.[21]

In recent revisions of baptismal rites throughout the Protestant traditions, the sign of the cross has been extended from use by the minister only with an invitation to others (such as godparents, family members and friends) to also take part in tracing it upon the one to be baptized. Similarly, in recent Catholic revisions, signing with the cross has been developed in light of practices recovered from fourth-century initiation celebrations, where the sign was employed and explained in rich detail. This has led to lavish contemporary expressions, such as in the *Rite of Christian Initiation of Adults* which includes various signations over the body:

Receive the sign of the cross on your forehead.
It is Christ himself who now strengthens you

with this sign of his love.
Learn to know him and follow him …
Receive the sign of the cross on your ears,
that you may hear the voice of the Lord.
Receive the sign of the cross on your eyes,
that you may see the glory of God.
Receive the sign of the cross on your lips,
that you may respond to the word of God.
Receive the sign of the cross over your heart,
that Christ may dwell there by faith.
Receive the sign of the cross on your shoulders,
that you may bear the gentle yoke of Christ.
Receive the sign of the cross on your hands,
that Christ may be known in the work which you do.
Receive the sign of the cross on your feet,
that you may walk in the way of Christ.[22]

This prayer is very clearly based on an extract from a sermon of the Cyril of Jerusalem, which is itself redolent of rich and extensive biblical images. He spoke to the recently baptized thus:

First you were anointed on the forehead so that you might lose the shame which Adam, the first transgressor, everywhere bore with him, so that you might 'with unveiled face behold the glory of the Lord' (2 Cor. 3.18). Next you were anointed on the ears, that you might acquire ears which hear those divine mysteries of which Isaiah said: 'The Lord has given me an ear to hear with' (Isa. 50.4). Again, the Lord Jesus in the gospel said: 'He who has ears, let him hear' (Matt. 11.15). Then you were anointed on the nostrils, so that after receiving the divine chrism you might say: 'We are the aroma of Christ to God among those who are being saved' (2 Cor. 2.15). After that, you were anointed on the chest, so that 'having put on the breastplate of righteousness, you might stand against the wiles of the devil' (Eph. 6.14, 11). Just as Christ after his baptism and visitation by the Holy Spirit went out and successfully wrestled with the enemy, so you also, after your holy baptism and sacramental anointing, put on the armour of the

Holy Spirit, confront the power of the enemy, and reduce it saying: 'I can do all things in Christ who strengthens me' (Phil. 4.13).[23]

While we have seen from this exploration of the gesture that the sign of the cross has had a variable history, so too has the *orans* posture. Although currently associated with Pentecostal and charismatic worship, and outside that context perhaps only with presidential prayer around the altar table (at least in many traditions), a remarkable study by John Leonard and Nathan Mitchell has uncovered the fact that the posture was sometimes, until the ninth century, adopted by whole congregations when celebrating the eucharist.[24] This is testified in one very powerful instance by illustrations accompanying the eighth-century *Drogo Sacramentary*. And in light of Leonard and Mitchell's findings, some strong arguments have recently been advanced for the recovery of the *orans* posture by the whole congregation throughout the eucharistic prayer. Richard Giles' *Creating Uncommon Worship* suggests that such a recovery would most fittingly express the calling of the whole assembly to fully participate in the liturgy, offering the prayer as co-celebrants with the presider.[25] A posture that has been partly recovered by the Pentecostal stream of Christianity may yet come to find more extensive use in wide styles of Christian worship.

Bowing is another gesture that repays careful attention. Although bows towards altar tables perhaps arose out of an earlier tradition associated with bowing to the east, bowing became a significant feature of Christian worship in the period in which basilicas were adopted as 'houses for the church', as this ritual gesture from the Roman law courts was transferred to new Christian usages of such buildings. The gesture is explicitly related in Roman Catholic understanding to the altar as symbol of Christ;[26] for example, the *Catechism of the Catholic Church* draws on the theology of Ambrose to assert that 'the Christian altar is the symbol of Christ himself, present in the midst of the assembly of his faithful'.[27] Many Christians of other traditions choose to partake in bows while enjoying greater freedom to construct the meaning of what they are doing. Some people may take the view that bowing towards an altar table is not appropriate after worshippers have ingested the elements of holy communion, for those who have received the eucharist may then themselves be regarded as the tabernacle of divine presence. Whether or not – and if, when – an altar table is reverenced communicates non-verbally important indicators about where Christ is believed to be present, and so where people may find and come to know Christ. So questions about the visual theology of ritual gestures may focus convictions of significance about the dignity bestowed by God upon God's beloved, and about graced lives being places of divine presence, activity and blessing.

Symbols and Scripture

Consideration of space and symbol can be a surprising context in which to find that the Bible itself, rather than being unrelated to liturgical symbolism, is so often the source of a great deal of the sign languages of worship. Indeed, 'the biblical foundations of Christian liturgy are more subtle than the obvious presence of the Bible' for not only are the scriptures present within the liturgy – read and preached, and in some liturgical styles processed, censed and kissed – it is partly through the symbolism of the liturgy itself, in whatever particular style, that scripture 'speaks' to worshippers. Gordon Lathrop writes that:

> Christian corporate worship is made up of chains of images: our gathering, our washing, our meal are held next to biblical stories, themselves read in interpretative chains, and this whole rebirth of images is itself biblical.[28]

In each liturgical celebration, as scripture is heard in juxtaposition to the symbols of the liturgy, we are presented with 'a skein of images reinterpreting images which is the very pattern of the gospel books themselves', so for example, in the lectionary's opening up of the scriptures, 'the mythic tree of Ezekiel 17, the tree in which the birds of the air all nest, the world tree, becomes the mustard bush of Mark 4.30–32'.[29] But this biblical dynamic is found throughout the liturgy, and is the way that liturgical symbols work:

> A similar skein is found every Sunday in the sanctus which takes the Song of the Cherubim from Isaiah 6 and sets it next to a verse from Psalm 118, reunderstood in the sense of the Jerusalem entry account in the Synoptic Gospels. Once again, by that very juxtaposition of image to image, a

rebirth occurs at the eucharistic event: the holy God seen in the temple, the pilgrims coming, the coming of Christ, this table – these are all made a chain. Thus the liturgy functions with the same skein that it has learned from the Bible itself.[30]

Scripture and symbol can be mutually reinforcing, and consciously and actively engaging in the symbolic dimensions of liturgy may indeed be a way of learning the Bible. Moreover, engaging symbols might even resist a 'biblical minimalism' that would run the risk of increasing 'subjective projection into the symbol (and, ironically onto the biblical texts themselves)'.[31] It is the alignment of word and gesture, the convergence of symbolic and cognitive suggestion that together form the multivalent environment of liturgical celebration. However, this does not make for simple kinds of certainties, but rather involves multivalent overlappings of meanings. A good example of this relates to the 'dispersal' of divine presence in the eucharist, noted in the last chapter, where we considered how the theology of *Sacrosanctum concilium* understands divine presence to be 'dispersed' among people, minister, word, sacramental action and sacramental element. All are affirmed as 'places' where 'Christ is present'. When, at the eucharist, bread is exchanged from one hand to another, with the words 'the body of Christ', the meaning is multivalent. That the bread is the body of Christ is one meaning of the words spoken, albeit the one which is, by many people, most immediately understood. However, the exchange is also itself the referent of the statement: the action is that of the body of Christ. Those alongside the speaker and hearer, the giver and receiver – or those surrounding them – are also the body of Christ. The entire assembly is the body of Christ. In part, what is understood by the exchange depends on how the words 'the body of Christ' are related to accompanying gestures. As Jan Michael Joncas notes, 'connotations depend on how the minister and recipient make eye contact, what tone of voice the minister uses, how the recipient articulates "Amen", and whether or not the host is placed on the hand or the tongue'.[32] Liturgical symbols speak because they *are* multivalent, and 'any attempt to reduce the[ir] significance to a single or preconceived meaning thwarts their efficacy'.[33]

Finally, liturgical symbols of course are also often closely intertwined with particular use of space. Space and symbol offer meaning to each other, just as both can each resonate scriptural meaning. A remarkable description of practices of penance from fifth-century Christian communities shows something of the interplay between space and symbol:

> The lot of the penitents was not a happy one, nor was it meant to be. Not only were they expected to demonstrate their remorse 'with downcast eyes and mournful faces', but they were also marked out as sinners by what they sometimes had to wear: sackcloth made of goat hair, to symbolize their separation from the sheep of Christ's flock; chains, to signify their bondage to sin; rags, to dramatize their poverty of virtue. Some had to cut their hair short like slaves, to show that they were slaves to Satan; others had to sprinkle themselves with ashes, to show they were spiritually dead like Adam, and cast out from the paradise of the church . . .
>
> As the penitential periods become longer, they were sometimes divided into several stages. In north Africa and other places in the West there were two stages in the penitential discipline: those who had not yet proven their willingness to reform their lives were treated like catechumens and dismissed after the sermon; those who had been officially admitted to ecclesiastical penitence could remain for the entire liturgy, but they were segregated from the rest of the congregation, and they could neither offer the gifts nor receive communion. In Asia Minor and other places in the East there were four grades in the order of penitents: 'weepers' had to remain outside the church and implore the prayers of the faithful; 'hearers' could stay at the back of the church, but only for the liturgy of the word; 'kneelers' could come further into the church and receive the bishop's blessing before being dismissed with the catechumens; 'standers' could remain for the entire liturgy but could not receive communion until they were restored to the status of communicant.[34]

Conclusion

In this chapter, we have considered space and symbol as two essential dimensions of liturgy. Both greatly influence the style of worship employed in every conceivable Christian tradition, and although not always acknowledged, both are immensely powerful means of participation in scripture and sacrament.

Further Reading

William Seth Adams, *Moving the Furniture: Liturgical Theory, Practice, and Environment* (New York: Church Publishing, 1999).

D. Foy Christopherson, *A Place of Encounter: Renewing Worship Spaces* (Minneapolis, MN: Augsburg Press, 2004).

Michael DeSanctis, *Building from Belief: Advance, Retreat and Compromise in the Remaking of Catholic Church Architecture* (Collegeville, MN: Liturgical Press, 2002).

Richard Giles, *Creating Uncommon Worship: Transforming the Liturgy of the Eucharist* (Norwich: Canterbury Press, 2004).

Richard Giles, *Re-Pitching the Tent: Re-Ordering the Church Building for Worship and Mission* (Norwich: Canterbury Press, 2004).

Richard Kieckhefer, *Theology in Stone: Church Architecture from Byzantium to Berkeley* (New York: Oxford University Press, 2004).

John K. Leonard and Nathan D. Mitchell, *The Postures of the Assembly During the Eucharistic Prayer* (Chicago, IL: Liturgy Training Publications, 1994).

David Philippart, *Saving Signs, Wondrous Words* (Chicago, IL: Liturgy Training Publications, 1994).

Phyllis Richardson, *New Sacred Architecture* (London: Laurence King Publishing, 2004).

Klemens Richter, *The Meaning of the Sacramental Symbols: Answers to Today's Questions* (Collegeville, MN: Liturgical Press, 1990).

R. Kevin Seasoltz, *A Sense of the Sacred: Theological Foundations of Christian Architecture and Art* (New York: Continuum, 2005)

James F. White, *The Cambridge Movement: The Ecclessiologists and the Gothic Revival* (Eugene, OR: Wipf and Stock Publishers, 2004).

James F. White, *Protestant Worship and Church Architecture: Theological and Historical Considerations* (Eugene, OR: Wipf and Stock Publishers, 2003).

James F. White and Susan J. White, *Church Architecture: Building and Renovating for Christian Worship* (Akron, OH: Order of St Luke, 1998).

3

Music and Song

How does music enrich words?
How do the psalms shape Christian worship?
How can music convey both intense feeling and deep emotion?
Can music express ambivalence towards God?

In this chapter we consider the role of music and song in Christian worship, noting different styles and uses of music in liturgy, and exploring the psalms as an enduring gift to the church's worship.

Different Uses of Music

Music and song are used in different ways in Christian worship. In some traditions mainly as accompaniment to liturgical action, the means by which a liturgical structure flows from one point to another. Though this happens in many different ways, an obvious example is the kind of 'mass setting' which enfolds the component elements of the eucharist in song: the Gloria, kyries, sanctus, and various acclamations – apart from other parts of the liturgy – may be sung. An interesting contemporary example of this use of music in the flow of the liturgy is Jaroslav Vadja's hymn 'Now the Silence' which is itself a meditation on the liturgical shape of the eucharist, moving through gathering, confession, absolution, sermon, preparation of the table, communion, and so on:

PREPARATION: Now the silence,
now the peace,
now the empty hands uplifted.

CONFESSION: Now the kneeling,
now the plea,
ABSOLUTION: now the Father's arms in welcome.

SERMON: Now the hearing,
now the power,
OFFERTORY: now the vessel brimmed for pouring.

COMMUNION: Now the body,
now the blood,
now the joyful celebration.

UNION WITH Now the wedding,
CHRIST now the songs,
now the heart forgiven leaping.

CHANNELS OF Now the Spirit's visitation,
GOD'S GRACE: now the Son's epiphany,
now the Father's blessing.

Now, now, now.[1]

It may be sung through, or used in sections to highlight particular points and transitions in the liturgical action.

In other traditions, music and song have a more expansive role than this, sometimes seen as the very heart of a style of worship. The great value placed on hymnody in Methodism is an obvious example – Gordon Wakefield's study of Methodist spirituality suggests that 'the influence of hymns on Methodism cannot be exaggerated'[2] – in which hymnody may be seen as opening up Christian experience, making theology available to the unschooled, and sustaining personal devotion as well as the praise of the gathered community. John Wesley, with his brother Charles, a founder of the Methodist movement, published many hymnbooks for the emerging Methodist people, and he referred to their main collection, of 1780, as 'a little body of experimental and practical divinity'.[3] Earlier, in 1761, he suggested some directives for the use of hymns in worship, and his ideas are very clearly indicative of his sense of how important singing is for shaping the faith of the congregation:

That this Part of Divine Worship may be more acceptable to God, as well as profitable to yourself and others, be careful to observe the following Directions:

1 Learn *these tunes* before you learn any others; afterwards learn as many as you please.
2 Sing them *exactly* as they are printed here, without altering or mending them at all; and if you have learned to sing them otherwise, unlearn it as soon as you can.
3 Sing *all*. See that you join with the congregation as frequently as you can. Let not the slight degree of weakness or weariness hinder you. If it is a cross to you, take it up and you will find a blessing.
4 Sing *lustily* and with good courage. Beware of singing as if you were half-dead, or half-asleep; but lift up your voice with strength. Be no more afraid of your voice now, nor more ashamed of its being heard, than when you sung the songs of Satan.
5 Sing *modestly*. Do not bawl so as to be heard above or distinct from the rest of the congregation; that you may not destroy the harmony; but strive to unite you voices together, so as to make one clear melodious sound.
6 Sing *in time*: whatever time is sung, be sure to keep with it. Do not run before or stay behind it; but attend close to the leading voices, and move therewith as exactly as you can. And take care you not sing *too slow*. This drawling way naturally steals on all who are lazy; and it is high time to drive it our from among us, and sing all our tunes just as quick as we did at first.
7 Above all sing *spiritually*. Have an eye to God in every word you sing.

Aim at pleasing him more than yourself, or any other creature. In order to do this attend strictly to the sense of what you sing and see that your *heart* is not carried away with the sound, but offered to God continually; so shall your singing be such as the Lord will approve of here, and reward when he cometh in the clouds of heaven.[4]

The role of the chorus in charismatic worship practice is another example of how song overflows its function in liturgical accompaniment, and might be considered constitutive of the tradition itself. It is at least very often the activity in which charismatic worshippers spend most of their time when they gather together.

As is the case with space and symbol, music and song are often close to the heart of participants' emotional engagement in worship. Musical dimensions of liturgy may express deeply felt devotion, and yet may also become a focus of gaping divisions within congregations.

The Psalms

The use of music in Christian worship of course has precedents in the faith of Israel. The Hebrew scriptures testify to the use of various instruments, of song and dance as expressions of praise. Central to this testimony is the book of Psalms, which continues to provide an important challenge and a test for contemporary music and song in worship.

We are mistaken to regard the psalms simply as notes of praise. They also embrace lament, despair and anger as well as the deepest joy. Don Saliers points out the 'full emotional range' of the psalms that embraces the wide breadth of human experience, or what Saliers calls in another place 'humanity at full stretch'.[5] It is this wide embrace of the breadth of human experience which enables those who recite and sing the psalms to know their own lives as 'places of encounter with God', and to resist limiting the sense of divine presence, God's concern for the human condition or involvement in human affairs to joyous feeling. The psalms may 'take us places we do not wish to go' as well as into 'luminous expanses of doxology',[6] and by so doing teach the reference of all things to God.

Moreover, it is the capacity of the psalms to embrace joy and sorrow that offers a particular way of relating to Jesus. For the psalms, of course, were the songbook of Jesus, and what the gospels suggest of his own use of the psalter underlines the demanding nature of its content, its potential to take its singers to places they may not wish to go. For it is in the horror of the cross where Jesus' own use of the psalms is most intense: two of the seven recorded words from the cross are in fact direct citations: 'My God, my God, why have you forsaken me?' (Ps. 22.1); 'Into your hands I commit my spirit' (Ps. 31.5). And in a fascinating and ancient apocryphal tradition, the expanse of joy and sorrow are blended in a most extraordinary way. Developing Mark 14.26, which tells us that on the night of the last supper, Jesus sang the psalms with the disciples and then left with them for the Mount of Olives, *The Acts of St John* elaborates:

Before he was arrested . . . he assembled us all and said, 'Before I am delivered to them, let us sing a hymn to the Father, and so go to meet what lies before us.' So he told us to form a circle, holding one another's hand, and himself stood in the middle and said, 'Answer Amen to me.' So he began to sing the hymn and to say, 'Glory be to thee, Father.' And we circled around him and answered him, 'Amen.'
'Glory be to thee, Logos; glory be to thee, Grace.' 'Amen.'
'Glory be to thee Spirit; glory be to thee, Holy One: glory be to thy glory.' 'Amen.'
'We praise thee, Father: we thank thee, Light, in whom darkness dwelleth not.' 'Amen.'
'And why we give thanks, I tell you: I will be saved, and I will save.' 'Amen.'
'I will be loosed, and I will loose.' 'Amen.'
'I will be wounded, and I will wound.' 'Amen' . . .
Grace dances. 'I will pipe, dance, all of you.' 'Amen.'
'I will mourn, beat you all your breasts.' 'Amen.'
'To the universe belongs the dancer.' 'Amen.'
'He who does not dance, does not knows what happens.' 'Amen' . . .
'I am a lamp to you who see me.' 'Amen.'
'I am a mirror to you who know me.' 'Amen.'
'I am a door to you who knock on me.' 'Amen.'

'I am a way for you, traveller.' 'Amen.'
'Now if you follow me, see yourself in me who am speaking, and when you have seen what I do, keep silence about my mysteries.' 'Amen.'
'You who dance, consider what I do, for yours is this Passion of Man which I am to suffer.' 'Amen' . . .
And after the Lord had so danced with us, my beloved, he went out. And we were . . . amazed . . .[7]

Vivifying the potential of the psalms to do their work is not helped by the monolithic way in which they are often employed in church. Unimaginative liturgical recitation or musical style, and particularly perhaps in some contexts unvarying use of Anglican chant, may be one of the least appropriate ways of employing the psalms in so far as they tend to 'flatten' the breadth of emotion expressed in the psalter, giving it all one tone and pace, harmonising the delight or torment that might be more apparent in another mode of any saying or singing psalms. Saliers rightly advises that 'we must continue to search for adequate musical forms and new translations of the texts' so that the 'emotional authenticity' of the psalter remains intact.[8]

Although the prayerbooks of many traditions provide translations of the psalms, most also allow any translation to be used in public worship. One way of opening up the diversity of expression in the psalms is, therefore, to use different translations. Something of what this might offer can be seen in the three contemporary psalm translations that follow, each presenting the opening verses of Psalm 34. First, the version produced for liturgical use by the International Commission for English in the Liturgy, aiming at 'a faithful and inclusive rendering of the Hebrew into contemporary English':[9]

I will never stop thanking God
with constant words of praise.
My soul will boast of God;
the poor will hear me and be glad.
Join me in praising the Lord,
together tell of God's name.
I asked and the Lord responded,
freed me from all my fears.

Turn to God, be bright with joy;
you shall never be let down.
I begged and God heard,
took my burdens from me.
God's angel defends the faithful,
guards them on every side.
Drink in the richness of God,
enjoy the strength of the Lord.
Live in awe of God, you saints:
you will want for nothing.
Even if lions go hungry,
those seeking God are fed . . . (Psalm 34.1–11)

Perhaps the most popular contemporary version of the psalms is Eugene Peterson's *The Message* paraphrase, in which he aims to correct the way in which many English translations, while 'superb in their scholarship', 'as prayers are not quite right'.[10] His own concern is to reflect the 'earthy and rough' prayer of the Hebrew psalter:

I bless Yahweh every chance I get;
My lungs expand with his praise.
I live and breathe Yahweh;
If things aren't going well, hear this and be happy:
Join me in spreading the news;
Together let's get the word out.
Yahweh met me more than halfway,
He freed me from my anxious fears.
Look at him; give him your warmest smile.
Never hide your feelings from him.
When I was desperate, I called out,
And Yahweh got me out of a tight spot.
Yahweh's angel sets up a circle
Of protection around us while we pray.
Open your mouth and taste, open your eyes and see –
How good Yahweh is.

Blessed are those who run to him.
Worship Yahweh if you want the best;
Worship opens doors to all his goodness.
Young lions on the prowl get hungry;
But Yahweh-seekers are full of God. (Psalm 34.1–11)

Juanita Colon was a Latino Manhattaner and Cistercian Sister who 'wrote the Psalms in her own words' for her own personal prayer, 'not withholding from God any of her own humanity'. She died in the middle of the fifth revision of her manuscript, which became available at her wake:

I will offer an unceasing litany of praise and glory to the Lord. The exalta-tion of my soul will instil new hope in the despairing. 'Yes, come', I will tell them; 'join me in singing praise to the Lord. Sing, friends, take heart! Don't be gloomy!' How I needed him: I called and called and then the answer came, peace came, deliverance from fear and anxiety. You can hope for this too, just turn to him for help and you'll find yourselves alight with joy. No more need to hide your faces in shame. Why, I know of someone desperate who cried out to God, was heard and saved. Yes, I know this man well. It is as if God sends angels to form a protective wall around his friends to repel all attack. Try him, see for yourselves how good he is and what happiness there is in store for those who rely solely on him. Revere the Lord, you his special friends; he loves you. What else do you need? The rich can lose everything in a second, be reduced to abject poverty and starvation, but God's friends – never. (Psalm 34.1–11)[11]

The way in which the psalms are said or sung matters because these ways concern, as Gabe Huck puts it, 'the way prayer gets into the voice'.[12] In *Music in Catholic Worship*, the Catholic Bishops of the United States wrote of the need that music in liturgy 'should heighten the texts so that they can speak more fully and more effectively', bringing 'the quality of joy and enthu-siasm which . . . cannot be gained in any other way'.[13] As Huck himself elaborates, music creates mood, and both expresses and deepens the atti-tude of those who enter into it.[14] And there is, perhaps, more: David Ford stresses a particular dimension of the action of singing itself – reflecting on

Ephesians 5.19–21, he writes of the capacity of song to actually and actively build up the Christian community, fostering unity: it 'encourage[s] alertness to others, immediate responsiveness to changes in tone, tune and rhythm, and sharing in the confidence that can come from joint singing. Singing together embodies joint responsibility in which each singer waits on the others, is attentive with the intention of serving the common harmony.'[15]

Conflict and Communion

Music in Christian worship can, however, be an arena of the most immense conflict. Congregations can define themselves by the songs they sing, or don't sing, just as they do by making conscious choices about the extent of their embrace of symbolism and gesture. Choice of song can be extremely telling, sometimes revealing either an inclusive or partisan approach to the community's identity.

Ideally, then, a breadth of song should be used. Carol Doran and Thomas Troeger, two North American hymnwriters and theologians, tell a story that yields a great deal of wisdom about how new music may affect those who sing it. They recount leading a workshop on music for a congregation, taking place over a weekend, culminating in Sunday morning worship. On the Saturday, they introduced a song that was new to the congregation, the Taizé chant 'Jesus, remember me when you come into your kingdom.' Yet despite being much appreciated by many members of the assembly, one man – entirely unfamiliar with this kind of repetitive, meditative song – was furious: 'You knew what you were doing', he accused the workshop leaders, as if they had intended to upset him.

Troeger and Doran conjecture that this man, who was someone usually concerned and able to take control of himself and his surroundings, had found himself disturbed to be singing 'tender music' and becoming 'visibly moved' before others. He had been unexpectedly drawn into expressing his own emotions. As Doran and Troeger suggest, 'we want to give ourselves to the music, but we fear what will happen if we do'.[16] And this reflects the reality of our engagement with the presence and demands of God upon our lives: 'we want to give ourselves to God, yet we fear what we happen if we do. These are more than parallel statements. The first is an expression of the second.' They go on to make a further link, which loops us back to our consideration of the psalms: whereas the psalms suggest the offering to God of a whole wealth of emotions – including the bleaker ones of fear and anger, and such like – most church music voices praise, but gives a great deal less voice to the bleaker realities of relating to God with the openness of the psalmists. And so 'as a result, our prayers, unlike the Bible, do not normally give expression to our ambivalence about God'. Through music, then, Troeger and Doran assert, we may be dealing with our relationship with God. A limited repertoire of music in liturgy may reflect only the more respectable dimensions of that relationship: our worthiness for acknowledging the 'worth-ship' (the root of the English word 'worship') of God, but very little of our private reserve and uncertainty. What meditative chants and repetitive choruses may do for some people is open up new space for the expression of emotion, either bleak or bright, that is more able to be contained in the singing of more cerebral hymnody.

Of course, quite obviously, not all choruses do express the realities of an 'ambivalent' relationship with the divine, and they can be the very worst cases of Christian song voicing only praise, without any of the shadows that are part of linking what is sung to our actual lives. Trite statements such as 'in his presence all our problems disappear'[17] is hardly a truthful statement about the life of faith and does little to reflect the stretch of the psalms. However, it is by no means the case that impoverished theology or confining ideas are contained only in new songs, or those of only particular Christian traditions and church styles. In light of ideas about psalms shaping Christian song, a particularly 'bad' theological use of the psalms is found in the traditional hymn, 'Father, hear the prayer we offer' by Love Maria Willis, which drastically subverts the meaning of Psalm 23, on whose images it draws so heavily:

> The Lord is my shepherd, I shall not want;
> he makes me lie down in green pastures.
> He leads me beside still waters ... (Psalm 23.1–2)

becomes, in the words of the hymn,

Not for ever in green pastures
do we ask our way to be:
but the steep and rugged pathway
may we tread rejoicingly.

Not for ever by still waters
would we idly rest and stay:
but would smite the living fountains
from the rocks along our way . . .

This, as Brian Wren points out, 'briskly set[s] the psalmist straight', offering a quite one-sided approach to Christian experience.[18]

Exploring the Chorus

Because they are increasingly popular, reckoning with the importance of the chorus in many churches' worship is an important task. Pete Ward's study of *Growing Up Evangelical* explores what recent generations of choruses have taught by the words they have given Christians to sing. His study makes clear the need for theological consideration of what gets into song, and what songs are used by the gathered Christian community. For instance, he finds in one of the first songbooks of the genre that is now so popular, *Youth Praise* of the 1960s, a concern to 'engage in a dialogue with youth culture'. There is both a concern for the 'unchurched' and 'a concrete feel about the need for outreach and the social implications of mission'.

Subsequent collections of choruses offered different theological accents and emphases: *Sounds of Living Water*, a popular songbook of charismatic renewal in the 1970s was, Ward suggests, marked by 'the feeling that is was important to gather together to be "filled" . . . joy in the fellowship of the body of the Church predominated'. This was in fact, and doubtless inadvertently, the start of a movement towards the marginalization of mission concerns. Moreover, in the 1980s collection *Songs of Fellowship*, 'an apocalyptic alarm begins to enter the vocabulary of the songs. The people of God gather for refuge'.[19] Ward is especially concerned to parallel the content of the songs in these various generations of new songbooks with the kinds of youthwork that evangelical churches – typically those who were using the songs – were at the same time offering to young people. In each generation, he finds significant parallels between the understanding of mission voiced in the songs and that embodied in the churches' youth ministries. Ward's fear is that choice of song – when it was perhaps not very discerning – was affecting the scope of mission in particular congregations – indeed, more than that, influencing whole ways of seeing the world. It is, of course, not simply that such songs were shaping the thinking of Christians, but also that particular kinds of songs may be more comfortably accommodated by congregations. The music assemblies sing needs to be stretching, both in its invitation to intimacy with the divine, and in robust engagement in the world. Ward's is an immensely powerful study of the importance of taking care what is sung, and why it matters.

As good examples of a contemporary hymn and a contemporary chorus, let me cite, first of all, Carl Daw's recent 'As Newborn Stars'. This hymn draws on a wealth of scriptural imagery to suggest what might be possible by way of employing the Bible in hymnody – though by no means employing it slavishly:

As newborn stars were stirred to song when all things came to be,
as Miriam and Moses sang when Israel was set free,
so music bursts unbidden forth when God-filled hearts rejoice,
to waken awe and gratitude and give mute faith a voice.

In psalms that raise the singer's sense to universal truths,
in prophet's dark-toned oracle or hymn of three brave youths:
the song of faith and praise endured through those God called to be
a chosen people bearing light for all the world to see.

When God's redeeming Word took flesh to make salvation sure,
unheeding hearts attuned to strife refused love's overture.
Yet to the end the song went on: a supper's parting hymn,
a psalm intoned on dying lips when sun and hope grew dim.

But silence won no victory there; a rest was all it scored
before glad alleluias rose to greet the risen Lord.
The church still keeps that song alive, for death has lost its sting,
and with the gift of life renewed the heart will ever sing.[20]

And a good example of a contemporary chorus is Matt Redman's 'The Friendship and the Fear', even the title of which gathers contrasting experiences of God:

You confide in those who fear You,
share the secrets of Your heart,
friendship give to those who seek to
honour you in every part.
Though I'm one of unclean lips, Lord,
I am crying 'Woe is me'
trying now to rid myself of
all the things than hinder me from

knowing You, hearing You speak,
seeing You move mysteriously.
Your whisperings in my soul's ear.
I want the friendship and the fear
of knowing You.

There is one thing You have spoken,
there are two things I have found;
You, O Lord, are always loving,
You, O Lord, are always strong.
I am longing to discover
both the closeness and the awe,
feel the nearness of Your whisper,
hear the glory of Your roar, just

knowing You, hearing You speak . . .[21]

One of the most exciting contemporary hymnwriters is Brian Wren, among whose widely sung work is the hymn of approach to the holy table, 'I come with joy to meet my Lord, forgiven, loved and free'. However, a number of

Wren's hymns are considerably more daring, suggesting fresh images of both the divine and of the human–divine relationship. For instance, one of his hymns draws its chorus from a saying of the medieval English mystic Julian of Norwich, whose 'revelations of divine love' included the assurance that 'all shall be well'. Around this refrain, it clusters extraordinary images of God: including 'gambler', who is to be found 'spinning the wheel of creation, giving it randomness, willing to be surprised, taking a million chances'. And it concentrates praise of God's faithfulness by use of the image of needle-craft: God 'watch[es] and patiently weav[es], quilting our histories, patching our sins with grace'. The hymn's praise of the strength of divine faithful-ness culminates in its startling affirmation that God 'danc[es] ahead of evil, kissing Satan's face, till all of our ends are wrapped in love's beginning'.

In another strange and interesting hymn, God – the 'name unknown, hidden and shown, knowing and known' – is praised in images related to those found in the Julian hymn. God is a 'spinner of chaos' and 'weaver of stories' who 'shapes a tapestry vivid and warm', as well as 'dare-devil gambler' and 'life-giving loser', who in Christ, 'wounded and weeping, dancing and leaping', crucified and risen, takes the risk of engagement with human beings, even to the extent of 'giving us freedom to shatter [God's] dreams'.[22] Hymns like these show how old and new can powerfully combine in contemporary expressions of praise.

Conclusion: Enrichment and Correction

Music and song are a major part of Christian worship, and are often close to the heart of a congregation's experience of liturgical renewal. Different kinds of music offer different things to those who sing them, perhaps even open-ing up different kinds of experience. Therefore, Brian Wren recommends 'a varied repertoire' of song in the liturgy, from a wide range of sources with diverse emphases, because this is as likely as anything to ensure that a full stretch of experience is articulated in both word and music:

If I sing it often enough to memorize it, the hymn will help to shape what I believe, and so either develop or distort my faith. The more I sing and enjoy it, the more it will encourage me to emphasize what it highlights and overlook what it hides. If I acquire a repertoire limited to devotional hymns about me and Jesus, in a worship setting with like limitations, it will not be surprising if I do not prioritise, or cannot express, joyful awareness of the Trinity, the Holy Spirit, God as wonderful creator, and the cosmic, social and historical scope of God's love. Conversely, if my repertoire is varied, one hymn's individual piety will be balanced by another's social conscience, and I can entrust myself to the viewpoint of the hymn I'm singing now, confident that it will be enriched, corrected, and supplemented by the next hymn I sing and by the hymns I sing next Sunday.[23]

The diverse repertoire he commends mirrors the diversity of the psalms.

Further Reading

Carol Doran and Thomas H. Troeger, *Trouble at the Table: Gathering the Tribes for Worship* (Nashville, TN: Abingdon Press, 1992).

Gail Ramshaw, *Words that Sing* (Chicago, IL: Liturgy Training Publications, 1992).

Don E. Saliers and Emily Saliers, *A Song to Sing, A Life to Live: Reflections on a Spiritual Discipline* (San Francisco, CA: Jossey-Bass, 2004).

Pete Ward, *Selling Worship: How What We Sing Has Changed the Church* (Carlisle: Paternoster Press, 2005).

Paul Westermeyer, *Te Deum: The Church and Music – A Textbook, a Reference, a History, and Essay* (Minneapolis, MN: Fortress Press, 1998).

Andrew Wilson-Dickson, *The Story of Christian Music: From Gregorian Chant to Black Gospel* (Minneapolis, MN: Fortress Press, 1996).

Brian Wren, *Piece Together Praise: A Theological Journey* (London: Stainer and Bell, 1996).

Brian Wren, *Praying Twice: The Music and Words of Congregational Song* (Louisville, KY: Westminster John Knox Press, 2000).

4

Discipleship and Learning: The Sermon

What are the challenges of preaching in our contemporary context?
What are the best ways of presenting biblical texts to the congregation?

Having considered the 'bones' of Christian worship, scripture and sacrament, which are 'enfleshed' by other aspects, such as space and symbol, music and song, we come in this final chapter of Part 1 to reflect upon the remaining pair of components of liturgy. Discipleship and learning relate particularly to the sermon, although, as we shall see in this chapter, contemporary liturgies invite a broad range of engagement with scripture.

Losing One's Words

O eternal Father! O fiery abyss of charity! O eternal beauty, O eternal wisdom, O eternal goodness, O eternal mercy! O hope and refuge of sinners! O immeasurable generosity! O eternal, infinite Good! O mad lover! . . . And what shall I say? I will stutter 'A-a', because there is nothing else I know how to say.[1]

Here, Catherine of Siena is lost for words, stuttering in wonder and amazement as she struggles to speak of the depths of divine reality. There are, of course, other reasons for being lost for words: Thomas Troeger, whom we met in the last chapter, suggests that contemporary preachers struggle, as they must, under the 'burden' of trying to 'carry the weight of the scriptural witness without help from the culture'. According to Troeger, unlike some of their preaching forebears, contemporary preachers may well now find themselves relating to listeners who are generally less biblically literate, or at least part of a society in which people do not imbibe in their ordinary ways of relating to one another and their world much of the scriptural imagery on which preaching draws. Finding words to help listeners relate their contemporary cultural perspectives to the Bible's modes and contents, may even, Troeger warns, mute preachers through 'burnout':

> Many articles have been written about burnout among the clergy. They usually address things like time management and the stress on ministers' families. Not for a moment would I deny these realities. But I sometimes think the greater cause is the spiritual exhaustion that develops as ministers realize the enormous gap between the gospel and the culture, the incessant tide of images, fads, and fashions that threatens to wash away the church's witness.[2]

So as well as highlighting some of the difficulty of preaching, this statement points to what it might cost those who try. We begin this chapter on preaching with Troeger's strong reminder of its contemporary context.

Ways to Preach a Sermon

There are, of course, many ways to preach a sermon. Preaching is sometimes categorized into different modes: expository, liturgical, pastoral, evangelistic, and so on; and each of these modes might itself range across wide styles of engaging with the Bible. A sample of the breadth of ways might include as one example – perhaps most obviously – something like John Stott's sense that preaching essentially involves 'translation' of a scriptural message:

> What is needed [in preaching] is a translation of the gospel into the language, idiom and thought forms of the modern world. But a genuine

translation is never a fresh composition; it is a faithful rendering into another language of something which has already been written or said.[3]

But there are perhaps more ways of being biblical than by doing direct interpretation of a biblical text,[4] and another style of preaching that might illustrate this well is something like Gail Ramshaw's delight in the biblical abundance of metaphor. Ramshaw suggests how preaching might play with metaphor, as different parts of scripture are juxtaposed, leading to 'skeins' of images to use the word of Gordon Lathrop. Ramshaw uses the Bible's freedom with metaphor as her encouragement to 'expand' the imagery Christians use to imagine, address and respond to the divine. And although she makes no claim that all the following images are biblical, and acknowledges that not all Christians would say 'yes' to all of the images she suggests – all beginning with just one letter of the alphabet, 'w' – she herself would say 'yes and no' for 'each might capture something of the mystery',[5] while each is also inadequate if it stands alone unaccompanied by other expansive images:

Waiter: one who serves, not 'Hi-I'm Suzie-I'm your-server', but black suit, elegant restaurant, unobtrusively, anticipating desires, meeting needs: God as waiter.

Washerwoman: a woman whose occupation is scrubbing recurring stains out of our sweaty clothes and our used sheets and our bloody towels: God as washerwoman.

Witch: one who with thoroughgoing knowledge of the forces of nature, the habits of creatures, and the patterns in plants has power to change what is to what is better: God as witch.

Wrestler: one who fought with Jacob long ago and with whom we contend still today, who at the end, after dislocating our limbs from their sockets, blesses us: God as wrestler.

Winter: a period of dormancy, appearing lifeless but nurturing renewal: God as winter.

Word: waves of sound connecting you and me, conveying part of myself to you; an I-love-you in the ear in the night: God as word.

Whaleboat: the rowboat in which we venture out to harpoon the whale, because we need oil for our lamps; a craft well designed to keep us afloat in dangerously high seas: God as whaleboat.

Wine: the centuries' old roots, the vine, the grapes, the juice, the chemical transformation, and finally the wine that gladdens the heart, lightens the mind, and unites the people at a table for two or a festivity for many: God as wine.

Wigwam: a circular family dwelling made of wooden poles and animal skins, handy for nomads to cart along as they travel: God as wigwam.

Womb: the dark warm matrix within which we curl up and grow; our seedpod, our sleeping bag: God as womb.

Watchtower: a phallic structure built on the edge of the city from which the sentries can spot the approaching enemy army: God as watchtower.

Woodworker: one who carves and whittles, measures and polishes, recreating trees into chairs and tables, beds and bookshelves, refashioning woodlands into wood for us: God as woodworker.

Wisdom: the goddess from ancient times who oversees the universe with justice and as tree of life offers superlative fruits for us to enjoy: God as wisdom.

Weapon: any of the many devices which protect me from harm by destroying it: God as weapon.

Way: Confucianism teaches that the way is straight and hierarchical, Taoism observes that the way meanders through the forest – which is it? God as way.

Whirlwind: wind turned wild, nature become preternatural, tearing Elijah away from Elisha and into heaven: God as whirlwind.

Wall: it keeps our snarling dog from attacking the neighbours: God as wall.

Wildfire: conflagration beyond comprehension; not as in the burning bush, a fire alive but not consuming, but blaze gone beserk – what's the purpose behind this uncontrollable destruction? God as wildfire.

Water: that which extinguishes fire; one of those very precious few things without which humans cannot long survive: God as water.

Winding sheet: swaddling clothes for a corpse, wrapping me round at death, keeping me together even then: God as winding sheet.

You stutter, looking for which w-w-words can begin to say God.[6]

Here, at the close of this riot of the imagination, she is recalling Catherine's 'stuttering', with which we began this chapter.

Opening the Scriptures

The issue of how the scriptures are presented to the assembly is inherently related to the style, quality and impact of preaching. Considering how to present the scriptures is of major importance because it determines to some extent the measure to which preaching can refer to the readings proclaimed, and whether or not listeners are required to recall the readings from memory, and whether or not they are enabled to set the readings in their canonical context.

A number of ways of presenting the scriptures are commonplace. The first is to free people from words on paper as much as possible, and to encourage good listening to the readings. This approach can be particularly important when literacy levels are low and the handling of books may be intimidating or off-putting, ill-fitting the local culture. It can also in some ways free worshippers from being 'text-bound' at a time when the general shift in liturgical style is towards the reduction of words on paper. If, in other parts of the liturgy, words on paper are used minimally, perhaps to clarify the structure and provide texts that are recited communally, but texts that require only one voice are not provided, it might seem incongruous to ask people to handle the biblical texts differently, particularly as many, if not most, scripture readings will simply be read aloud by a single voice. If notice of the readings for each forthcoming Sunday can be given on the preceding week's notice-sheet, people can be encouraged to read the scriptures that will be used in the assembly in the days leading to the Sunday gathering. And in the assembly itself, attentive listening can be encouraged in a number of ways: standing to listen to at least some of the readings shifts people into a posture in which they enact their being called to attention. Generous, unhurried silence following each reading allows the verses to 'echo', as it were, as the texts are personally appropriated. And use of silence can in turn be encouraged and enhanced by use of simple bell-sounds as cues to call people out of their personal reflection back to gathered attentiveness to the next reading. Some churches use bells more ambitiously around scripture readings, using the long sonorous note of a Buddhist-type prayer bowl to invite silence after reading and again to end silence as the liturgical movement shifts to the next focus of attention.[7] Such things may indeed enrich the liturgy, but neverthe-less the absence of the text for people and preacher to refer to during the sermon may remain a weakness of this approach.

A second way of presenting the scriptures is to introduce lectionary books. These collect and present in sequence the readings for each given Sunday. Worshippers may then turn to the page at which readings for the particular day begin and follow them through as they are read aloud to the assembly. An advantage of this approach is that people are not required to root out a number of readings from different parts of the Bible, which might be con-sidered a distraction or a challenge, particularly in sequences which include obscure minor prophets and so on. However, this approach may unnecessar-ily tie congregations down to the suggested set readings for each Sunday and discourage the construction of local lectionaries.[8]

An increasingly common option, because of the ease of photocopying, is now to print out readings on a weekly 'flyer' inserted in the notice-sheet. Materials of this kind can be either bought in or locally produced, though the latter may prove time-consuming (although perhaps a good Lenten discipline for volunteer typists!). However, both this and the previous way of presenting the scriptures suffer from the serious weakness of severing the Sunday read-ings from their canonical context, the form in which worshippers are most likely, if at all, to engage with scripture outside the gathered congregation. For this reason, perhaps the best means of presenting the scriptures on Sundays is to invite the congregation to handle copies of the Bible. This approach, of course, requires considerable thought about its accessibility (especially to visitors). At the very least page numbers need to be given out as well as book, chapter and verse references. This kind of information can, however, easily be given on the Sunday notice-sheet, and indeed, any verbal notices in the service (if announced at the beginning) can give out page numbers of the readings and time can be made at that moment to mark the pages with ribbons so as to avoid the possible distraction of searching and turning over pages between the readings. This would make the literal handling of scripture something that happened as part of the gathering of God's people, and thus could itself be a strong symbolic statement about gathering to attend to the sources of the Christian story which shape the assembly. Also, worshippers having Bibles in their hands as the sermon is preached allows the preacher to cross-reference to other parts of the scriptures as she or he is proclaiming the gospel and may also strengthen the link between preaching and teaching. Whether or not this facility is considered to be valuable may depend on the preacher's and listeners' prior convictions about what the sermon is in fact an opportunity for. Yet the principal merit of worshippers handling Bibles for themselves remains, as it enables the assembly of the church to be a place where the handling of scripture can – if it is done well – be learned, especially as there may be few other contexts in which the basic skills of Bible reading are appropriated. In short, if biblical literacy is not nurtured 'in church', where will it be?

How best to negotiate the options will differ from place to place, but the conviction of this book is that the latter of the various suggestions explored here is the most appropriate means of encouraging biblical literacy in our cultural context.

A Range of Opportunities for Learning

We have noted there are many ways to preach a sermon, and recognized that how the scriptures are presented to the assembly may to some extent determine what is possible by way of preaching. It is also important to note the growing encouragement of the various churches to engage and respond to the 'umbrella culture'. For instance, the *Methodist Worship Book* suggests that in the service of holy communion 'God's word is proclaimed and shared in songs, hymns, music, dance and other art forms, in a sermon, or in comment, discussion and in silence'.[9] Likewise, *Common Worship* suggests that 'the term "sermon" includes less formal exposition, the use of drama, interviews, discussion, audio-visuals and the insertion of hymns or other sections of the service between parts of the sermon' which may come before or after one of the readings or prayers.[10] In each case, the sermon (in the narrow sense) is only one means of engaging the word, and a whole ecology of ways of appropriating and responding to scripture is suggested. This diversification of means of communication and appropriation is increasingly important in order to help people to hear and respond to the scriptures. Yet this in itself may not be enough. Home groups and study groups, and in some places, all-age Sunday school classes may be essential to support lifelong learning in the faith.

Home groups and study classes are one means by which the monological sermon might be expanded, although there are also tested ways of bringing a more dialogical approach into the Sunday assembly. For instance, the readings from scripture might be followed by a simple questions such as 'How do you respond to this reading?', inviting the contributions of members of the assembly, which a skilful preacher can scoop up and use in his or her monologue which follows at the end of the sequence of readings and responses. Otherwise, some discussion might follow at the end of a monological sermon, opened by a question such as 'Does anyone want to make a comment, ask a question, tell a story or share a picture that has come to mind in the light of God's word today?' In this case, the preacher might briefly respond to each comment, and also claim the last word, as it were, rounding off the fragments that have been contributed by others. Welcoming responses either to the readings before a sermon, or during the sermon may require some quick thinking on the part of preachers but is likely to lead to a richer liturgy of the word, in which a number of voices actively participate. The conversational style of this aspect of the liturgy might also happily mirror a healthy understanding of the Bible itself – a collection of books – as more like a complex and inviting conversation than a divine monologue that can be appropriated simplistically.

Yet despite all the ways in which the monological sermon might be supplemented and enriched, it is important not to forget, in the words of William Willimon, 'the simple, stunning beauty of one human being, standing up before fellow human beings, clearing her throat, and daring to speak'.[11] And in the light of the 'new' approaches to preaching suggested in the previous paragraphs, it is reassuring to hear from Willimon that the sermon preached by just one voice in fact always involves an element of dialogue:

One of the beautiful things about preaching within the congregation, as opposed to preaching on the radio or television, is that this is your pastor, the person who lives where you live. This isn't a religious address which is delivered to all . . . in general. This is the word for the folk at your church, born out of the intersection between the pastor's Bible study and the pastor's care of the congregation. So there is a sense in which you have been helping your pastor to write the sermon all week long. The word you hear is the word which your pastor is convinced needs to be said within this congregation which stands under the word of God . . .[12]

As well as affirming the continuing role of the more traditional understanding of the sermon, this statement might also bestow confidence to expand the dialogue that is, according to Willimon, always inherently present.

Life-Giving Preaching

When William Willimon writes about the purpose of preaching, he is quite clear about its work in the assembly:

Without the sermon, there is always the danger that our liturgy might degenerate into an escape, a fantasy trip out of the cares of this world into some never-never land where pain is not really pain, decisions are not really difficult, and life floats above any cares or problems. Without this contemporary word, this present testimony of the faith, we might all simply gather, pat one another on the back, smile, sail off into our dreams, and then go back home no different than when we came.

The sermon is our primary protection against such infidelity.[13]

Preaching is about directing people to the fullness of life God intends for human beings, which most certainly requires an 'ethical bent' to the call to discipleship. For Willimon, the sermon is at least in part about 'following' as opposed to simply 'admiring' Jesus. It introduces the otherness of scripture and its perspectives, not least those of its focal character, Christ Jesus, and so resists worship being engaged simply on worshippers' terms, with all the limitations of a solely contemporary perspective.

Marva Dawn also insists on this dimension to discipleship, which preaching should proclaim. Following Jesus involves responding to demands that may be stretching. In Dawn's arresting phrase, 'worship ought to kill us': 'Everything we do in worship should kill us, but especially the parts of the service in which we hear the Word – the Scripture lessons and the sermon.'[14] The death to which she refers is of course of 'sin' and 'self-centredness', which require the kind of 'crucifixion with Christ' (Gal. 2.19–20) which 'allows us to be born anew to worship God rightly'.[15] For Dawn, 'The goal of preaching to train listeners to be theologians prohibits the sermon from being mere triviality or entertainment' and must have the ethical bent of which Willimon also speaks. Dawn points us towards the enfleshment of the word in the performance of scripture, as she relates this vignette:

> 'Pastor, that was a wonderful sermon,' said the parishioner at the door after the service.
> 'That remains to be seen,' said the preacher[16]

the preacher's point being that the content of 'wonderful sermons' need to be enacted in worshippers' lives. This conviction mirrors the current popularity of 'performance' as something of a keyword in theories of biblical interpretation,[17] and locates the ultimate authority of scripture in the convincingness of the ways it is lived and fosters human flourishing.

Perhaps not only scripture, but preaching itself can be performed in this sense, as may be seen in this oft-quoted, yet still fresh, rabbinical anecdote:

> A rabbi, whose grandfather had been a disciple of the Baal Schem, was asked to tell a story. 'A story', he said, 'must be told in such a way that it constitutes help in itself.' And he tells: 'My grandfather was lame. Only they asked him to tell a story about his teacher. And he related how the holy Baal Schem used to hop and dance while he prayed. My grandfather rose as he spoke, and he was so swept away by his story that he himself began to hop and dance to show how the master had done. From that hour he was cured of his lameness. That's the way to tell a story!'[18]

This remarkable anecdote underscores how much it matters that preaching is 'performed', in the sense of words being enacted in living, and its reference to dance is a reminder of an activity in which it is common to join in. It also suggests that preaching may have a vital part to play in enabling worship to bring about transformation, to open up fullness of life. And having considered the shape of Christian worship in Part 1, it is to the range of human life, its cultures, cycles, crises and needs that we now turn in Part 2, 'Worship and Mission in a Diverse World'.

Further Reading

David Buttrick, *Homiletic: Moves and Structures* (Minneapolis, MN: Fortress Press, 1987).

David Day, *A Preaching Workbook* (Eastbourne: Lynx, 1995).

David Day, Jeff Astley and Leslie J. Francis (eds), *A Reader on Preaching: Making Connections* (Aldershot: Ashgate, 2005).

Susan Durber and Heather Walton (eds), *Silence in Heaven: A Book of Women's Preaching* (London: SCM Press, 1994).

Mary Catherine Hilkert, *Naming Grace: Preaching and the Sacramental Imagination* (New York: Continuum, 1997).

Thomas G. Long, *Testimony: Talking Ourselves Into Being Christian* (San Francisco, CA: Jossey-Bass, 2004).

Thomas G. Long, *The Witness of Preaching* (Louisville, KY: Westminster John Knox Press, 1990).

Gail Ramshaw, *Treasures Old and New: Images in the Lectionary* (Minneapolis, MN: Fortress Press, 2002).

Stanley P. Saunders and Charles L. Campbell, *The Word on the Street: Performing the Scriptures in an Urban Context* (Grand Rapids, MI: Eerdmans, 1999).

Thomas H. Troeger, *Imagining a Sermon* (Nashville, TN: Abingdon Press, 1990).

Thomas H. Troeger, *Preaching while the Church Is Under Reconstruction: The Visionary Role of Preachers in a Fragmented World* (Nashville, TN: Abingdon Press, 1999).

Fritz West, *Scripture and Memory: The Ecumenical Hermeneutic of the Three-Year Lectionaries* (Collegeville, MN: Liturgical Press, 1997).

Part 2

Worship and Mission in a Diverse World

Whereas Part 1 of this book was concerned with the various component parts of Christian worship across a wide range of traditions, the focus in Part 2 turns to matters of mission. This expands attention to things already considered. Its range is wider than Part 1 in that:

Chapter 5 surveys new challenges in liturgical study and points to current and future developments. In stressing the importance of inclusivity in the Christian assembly, it complements Part 1's emphasis on convergence, but it also links inclusivity to the church's witness.

Chapter 6 explores some of the many ways in which liturgy relates to time. Both cycles (such as the liturgical year) and crises – key times in the human life-cycle – are considered. The chapter suggests that the seven sacraments of Catholic tradition, each of which is transposed in some way into Protestant worship, are a major means by which liturgy gives particular shape to human life.

Finally, Chapter 7 sketches some contours of a 'liturgical spirituality', exploring how engagement in Christian worship nurtures human maturity. There are several foci in the chapter, but it concludes with a focus on the eucharist, where we began at the opening of Part 1.

5

Styles and Substance: Celebrating Diversity

How does worship evangelize?
Is diversity in worship more a threat or a promise?
How do marginal styles of Christian worship contest the ecumenical liturgical consensus?

In this first chapter in our explorations of 'Worship and Mission in a Diverse World' we survey the rich diversity of contemporary expressions of worship. As it unfolds, the chapter touches on various attempts to relate worship and evangelism, and it attends to the perspectives of a number of theologies and spiritualities which are inviting engagement with liturgical studies: feminist, postcolonial and queer. Some of the issues introduced in the chapter are decidedly 'new', such that the churches' official liturgical revisions are not yet, or are only just becoming conscious of the challenges they present. In the case of some of the issues under consideration, it is yet to be seen how the churches' worship resources will come to be shaped differently because of them. At the very least in addressing new issues and attending to contemporary concerns reflects the fact that liturgy is by no means a static reality. Close to the heart of the liturgy itself, in the ways that divine presence is associated with the very matter of the sacraments – 'fluid, or consumable, transient, except in their immediate or longer term effects on the persons concerned, themselves the pilgrims'[1] – we find good reason for valuing fresh things.

Convergence and Diversity

In Chapter 1, we celebrated the convergence of styles of worship across a range of Christian traditions. We saw that much of this convergence was related to the recovery of Justin Martyr and other early writers' witness to the shape of the liturgy in the first centuries of the church. However, convergence is only one – although, at the moment, the major – part of contemporary liturgical developments. For instance, it remains the case that many Christians worship in styles that simply do not reflect the pattern of gathering, word, table, sending. Some kinds of Pentecostal worship may not always, or ever, follow this fourfold pattern.

The Pentecostal tradition is one of the newer of those enduring Protestant styles of church that have emerged since the Reformation. In his book *Protestant Worship*, James White points out that for the 50 years following 1520, five new traditions came into being: the Lutheran, Reformed, Anabaptist, Anglican and Puritan traditions. He adds that since 1590, major new traditions have emerged roughly at the rate of one a century, as opposed to one a decade, with the flourishing of Quaker in the seventeenth, Methodist in the eighteenth, Frontier in the nineteenth, and Pentecostal traditions in the twentieth centuries.[2] White views this diversity positively, understanding the growth of the Protestant churches as itself a testimony to the sheer richness of Christian worship.

Echoing White's insight, there is a widening interest in appreciating marginal traditions in their similarities to and differences from the shared aspects many churches embrace in their liturgies. For instance, the World Council of Churches has recently made conscious and concerted efforts to acknowledge and include the 'new' traditions of Pentecostal and radical-Reformation heritage in its dialogue about worship.[3] Alongside these developments which recognize diversity in Protestant traditions, it is important to remember that, as James White argues in another place,[4] the Roman Catholic tradition has been far from static or homogeneous throughout the centuries.

Seeker Services

One important point to make about diverse styles of Christian worship is that they ought to allow greater numbers of people to join in. That is, they ought to allow for people to find something of their own preferences (perhaps in style of music, for instance) reflected in one of many ways of worship. This kind of assertion underlies the attempts of increasing numbers of church communities to develop 'seeker services' that might appeal particularly to those for whom 'traditional' services of worship seem to hold little appeal. In fact, a 'seeker service' movement has grown out of the Frontier tradition and has spawned a multitude of both small-scale projects and world-renowned examples such as the Willow Creek enterprise in the United States. Character-istics of these various modes of seeker-friendly experiences of church often seem to include: a reduced diet of scripture, perhaps not expounded by a preacher; an absence of sacraments; a setting in a context which may resem-ble a theatre or cinema rather than a building shaped by the tradition of space used for Christian worship; and perhaps also an event purged of com-munal action and song, and hosted by a 'master of ceremonies' type-figure perhaps modelled on the role of the television presenter.

In the case of Willow Creek, events with these kinds of characteristics grew out of some limited, but powerful, 'market research' that tried to respond to the fact that young men between 25 and 50 are often absent from church. Bill Hybels, the founder of the Willow Creek Community, took a number of colleagues door-to-door to ask men directly what it was about church services they found off-putting, in order to think about what a redress to their perceptions might be.

They wanted to know if the residents went to church, and if not, why not. They summarized the responses in five statements:

1 Churches are always asking for money (yet nothing significant seems to be happening through the use of the money).
2 Church services are boring and lifeless.
3 Church services are predictable and repetitive.
4 Sermons are irrelevant to daily life as it is lived in the real world.

5 The pastor makes people feel guilty and ignorant, so they leave church
  feeling worse than when they entered the church doors.[5]

Whatever the limitations of the their particular research method, and their
placement in one particular cultural context, their sense of the 'problems'
many men (and others) have about worship demand the best attention of
Christian communities in every tradition and circumstance.

The development of 'seeker services' in recent decades have been one
attempt by churches to inhabit the dominant culture in ways that might be
more comfortable to initial enquirers after Christian faith. Their development represents not only an enormous challenge, but has also been subject
to question and critique. For instance, in 'seeker service' circles, concern is
sometimes expressed that the pattern of gathering, word, table and sending
does not relate at all well to some aspects of dominant western cultures. The
very idea of gathering might be challenging in a highly individualistic society
– let alone gathering around scripture, which may be highly inaccessible to
people with no previous teaching about it, or sacraments which may be very
unfamiliar and much misunderstood. Some contemporary missiologists
argue that 'congregational dynamics' are problematic in contemporary culture, and that effectively engaging participants in contemporary culture will
require offering ways of expressing faith that are less dependent on gathering
with others.[6]

In Britain, although not always adopting the designation 'seeker service',
worship that is marked by some if not all of these characteristics is often
presented as 'family worship', 'all-age worship', 'alternative worship' or worship
particularly accessible to the young. And because to some extent these quite
consciously mirror aspects of popular entertainment culture, they often are
widely appreciated and enjoyed. However, although such endeavours involve
obvious and welcome moves to make Christian worship accessible, at the
same time they raise many important questions about 'what is essential in
Christian worship'.[7] For instance, are particular types of building or presidency essential? Should content be shaped by sacrament and scripture? Must
there be an emphasis on participation, and how is this to be achieved in space
shaped for the consumption of certain kinds of entertainment? Such questions challenge not only those for whom 'seeker services' appeal, they can also

reveal how little participation actually goes on, and how the central things of scripture and sacrament may not shape a congregation's consciousness of worship. For liturgical theologians at least, the seeker service movement has raised questions about what Christian worship celebrates that is distinct from contemporary cultural forms, how that distinctiveness is made central, and what kind of liturgical elements are necessary to ensure the distinction. At the very least, Christian worship does not simply celebrate 'celebration' as an end in itself, as psychologist of religion Paul Pruyser asserts in a biting critique of some contemporary modes of worship he regards as vacuous:

> In casting our eyes on the current religious scene we should be arrested by the sudden popularity that the word celebration has gained. The religious world today seems full of joyful noises and happenings. Or should I say that it is full of strenuous talk about these desirable things and replete with strained efforts to produce them, often with rather hapless results? . . . I see a wide gap, however, between wishing to celebrate and knowing what to celebrate; the cart seems to be put before the horse. A wish to celebrate may come from sheer boredom; it is a longing for affective experience per se, which may prompt one to going through the celebratory motions so as to capture some emotion. It is like saying with a yawn, 'Let's have a party!' without having an occasion, reason or disposition for one.[8]

Other views offer more constructive proposals, as in Gordon Lathrop's argument that it is essential scripture and sacrament are central to styles of worship which would claim the title 'Christian', because 'the life-giving presence of God is actually given in word and sacrament'. He explains, 'without the stories of the Scriptures, without "this is my body, given for you," without the living water of baptism, this talk can be hazy, unhelpful, perhaps Gnostic, often simply code words for the self'.[9] This kind of reserve about the marginalization of sacrament and scripture, and its assertion about what scripture and sacrament promise, is a powerful challenge to any simple affirmation of the need for worship to be culturally accessible.

While at least some of the shifts embraced by the seeker-service movement have influenced patterns of worship in the mainline churches, and while wanting to take the challenges presented by contemporary culture seriously, the kinds of approach developed by Willow Creek have by and large been discouraged by mainstream or old-line churches, although not always by means of theological arguments like Lathrop's. Perhaps the mainstream traditions have usually maintained some measure of resistance to the consumerist culture with which Willow Creek is decidedly more comfortable? This does not mean, though, that the churches have simply reiterated their received traditions of worship.

Directory Approaches to Liturgy

While not embracing the methods of 'seeker services' emerging in recent years out of the American Frontier tradition, mainstream traditions have sometimes been greatly concerned to reappraise their approach to their liturgical inheritance in order that worship might better serve contemporary evangelism. For instance, the Church of England has been greatly concerned to develop fresh ways of organizing liturgy and providing liturgical resources. Received patterns have been especially critiqued from two angles – the situation of urban churches, and the quest to involve the young in worship. *Faith in the City*, described by some as the most important Anglican document of the twentieth century,[10] made a number of biting criticisms of inherited Anglican liturgical forms, perhaps most notably its suggestion that 'a 1300 page Alternative Service Book is a symptom of the gulf between the Church and ordinary people' in underdeveloped urban areas.[11] Donald Gray, then chair of the Church of England's liturgical commission, concurred that the church's liturgical resources had very often been 'blunt instruments of evangelism'[12] in urban and other contexts.

Other reports, such as *Youth-A-Part*, identified young people's widely articulated problems with inherited styles of worship as one factor in the need for 'a change in the overall culture' of church if young people are to embrace it,[13] and reports on the church's mission among children called for 'new liturgies to serve all-age worship and in particular a form of Eucharist suitable for when children are present'.[14] A key result of these critiques has been *New Patterns for Worship* which has incorporated two novel developments in English Anglican liturgy: its rich 'directory' of resources and an extensive 'commentary' intended to help worship leaders prepare and preside in worship in new ways. *New Patterns for Worship* is essentially a new kind of prayerbook for the Church of England.[15]

New Patterns for Worship was published in a series of experimental drafts in the late 1980s and 1990s and was consciously developed to respond to the expressed needs of urban and young persons. It was intended to provide greater freedom by expanding the bounds of local choice more widely than had been customary in English Anglican tradition, by providing variable texts that might be used to enrich and shorten services – though at the same time to clarify liturgical frameworks so that the range of new freedoms might retain common characteristics. By the time the prayerbook was published in its final form in 2002, the kind of approach it had developed to the needs of the young and to urban persons had so influenced the way in which the Church of England was coming to think about its liturgy that the definitive edition expressed the aim of 'educat[ing] and train[ing] those who plan and lead worship'[16] across the *Common Worship* range. Its intended aims are to teach how to construct particular celebrations, to encourage seasonal and other variation and to show how local orders might be developed. *New Patterns for Worship* is organized into four sections:

- *The Introduction* is mainly given to stories of 'four imaginary churches' which are central to the book's teaching role. The four churches describe very different kinds of congregations in different settings and with different styles. One of the four churches – St Dodo's – is, as the name suggests, an example of how not to do liturgy. It counsels those whose experience resonates with St Dodo's not to despair: 'you're not extinct yet, and the fact that you are using this book shows that you are well on the way to recovering from deadness'.[17]
- *Planning Worship* is a large section which again uses stories from the four churches to illustrate the principles of liturgy that *Common Worship* enshrines. This section includes material that is repeated in the *Common Worship* Sunday book, including the service of the word, which is comprised entirely of shape and rubrics – with no set texts whatsoever. It also includes material on space, colour, music, etc. – aspects of liturgy beyond the text.

- *Resource Sections* constitute the main part of the book arranged thematically around: gathering and greeting, penitence, praise and thanksgiving, the peace, and other aspects of worship. This is the directory from which material can be drawn and arranged by liturgical leaders according to the principles outlined in the material on 'Planning Worship'. This section includes some particularly notable material on using the lectionary.

- *Sample Services* The final part is a series of 'sample services' that show in practice how the directory might be used to create worship according to the principles espoused. One example service (called 'All Creation Worship') suggests both a people's text and a minister's text: the people's order is for use by the congregation, and includes only the structure, rubrics and texts for prayer they actually need, while the minister's text has all the words of the service, most of which are not needed by the congregation at all. The minister's text, of course, looks much more like a Book of Common Prayer service, including all the words, whereas what the people have in their hands is only what they need to participate.

Clearly, *New Patterns for Worship* has involved a re-evaluation of the Anglican inheritance of worship and particularly a rethinking of the notion of 'common prayer'. While Anglican tradition once required use of the Book of Common Prayer or other subsequent prayerbooks which were arranged in prescriptive ways, the new directory approach to liturgical resources means that common prayer can no longer involve narrowly prescriptive use of set texts, but rather the notion of common prayer is centred around a number of marks felt to characterize the Anglican liturgical tradition. These are said to be:

- a recognizable structure for worship;
- an emphasis on reading the word and on using psalms;
- liturgical words repeated by the congregation, some of which, like the creed, would be known by heart;
- using a collect, the Lord's prayer, and some responsive forms in prayer;
- a recognition of the centrality of the eucharist;
- a concern for form, dignity, and economy of words;
- a willingness to use forms and prayers which can be used across a broad spectrum of Christian belief.[18]

Among other things, this statement affirms both the centrality of word and sacrament, and the kind of 'recognizable structure' of which gathering, word, table, sending is the most obvious. And for the mainline or old-line churches at least, *New Patterns for Worship* may suggest a way that many other traditions will employ as they come to revise their own liturgical resources, particularly given the massive technological advances – especially in computing – that have enabled congregations very easily to develop local orders of service.

Pentecostal/Charismatic Style

The Pentecostal tradition has seen exponential growth throughout the world since the early twentieth century. The tradition emerged out of a poor urban community in Los Angeles in the 1900s and was marked, particularly in its early years, by interethnic gathering for worship that was radical in its time and place. Since those beginnings, Pentecostalism has emerged in a number of waves, the second of which, in contrast to its egalitarian origins became 'segregationalist, individualistic, culture-bound and inward-looking',[19] so that the social radicalism of the early years was severely diminished. The third wave is sometimes referred to as 'charismatic' and is associated with the period since the 1970s when many features of worship in the Pentecostal tradition have increasingly come to enjoy a measure of integration in the worship styles of older traditions.

Some of these features include words of knowledge, prophecy and prayer for healing, all activities believed to be in line with practices witnessed in the Corinthian church to which two New Testament letters are addressed, and where these practices are understood as 'gifts of the Spirit'. Another gift in evidence in Corinth was speaking in tongues, and it is this that is perhaps the most distinctive mark of classical Pentecostal worship and spirituality. Many Pentecostals have believed the giftedness to speak in tongues to be the necessary evidence of 'baptism in the Holy Spirit', and for many Pentecostals this tongue-speaking is central to the ways in which they themselves believe they are distinguished from other Christians. While speaking in tongues remains a strange notion to some contemporary Christians, its appropriation into charismatic worship in the wider liturgical tradition of historic denominations has 'normalized' it for others.

Gray Temple, an American Anglican charismatic, here gives testimony to his first experience of tongue-speaking and some of the other Pentecostal gifts:

[Bill] asked Helen to pray over him, using glossalalia. She did so – and I understood what she'd said! This was my first exposure to someone speaking or praying with tongues, and it startled me to have it seem natural. When I reported my interpretation of Helen's prayer to him, he jumped with surprise. My words seemed non-specific to me, but something in them grabbed him personally . . . without the others knowing it. So I dropped to my knees and asked Helen to do the same thing for me. She did. Bill understood it. He reported to me that Jesus was entering me with some badly needed soothing gentleness – sopping up a lot of rage I'd been plagued with over recent years – promising that my life would come to be a continual *Te Deum Laudamus*. (The latter is a chant Episcopalians sometimes use in worship. Bill couldn't have known that it's my favourite bit in the Prayer Book). The message was clear . . .[20]

As Harvey Cox comments:

Tongue speaking is an ecstatic experience, one in which the cognitive grids and perceptual barriers that normally prevent people from opening themselves to deeper insights and exultant feelings, are temporaly suspended.

Ecstasy, as my late teacher, the theologian Paul Tillich, wrote, is not an irrational state. It is a way of knowing that transcends everyday awareness, one in which 'deep speaks to deep' . . .[21]

Although these activities are those with which particular biblical correlations tend to be made, a number of other features characterize Pentecostal worship, notably high levels of emotional display, lively, highly celebratory music – often danced as well as sung to – and extempore prayer. Yet Pentecostal worship style is better described as 'informal' than 'spontaneous', for deep patterns are often embedded within it, as Walter Hollenweger observes:

An ocean of faces floated before my eyes, 2000 to 3000 faithful, some with car-tyres on their feet instead of shoes. But as soon as the trumpet blew the first melody, those faces, creased with the sign of age-long oppression, came to life. In a circle the people danced slowly the dances of their Indian ancestors. Those who did not dance stood reverently and clapped their hands slowly. A woman prophesied in a deep, soul-searching voice. All of a sudden there was silence! The whole congregation fell down on their knees in order to thank God for the dance he had given them . . . The most important element of the Pentecostal worship is the active participation of every member of the congregation, even if this amounts to several thousand people . . . In the structure of the Pentecostal liturgy one might find most of the elements of historical liturgies: Invocation, Kyrie, Confession, Gloria, Eucharistic Canon and Benediction. Yet these parts are hardly ever so named . . . [They are linked together with the help of] so-called choruses, i.e. short spontaneous songs, known by heart by the whole congregation . . . If someone sings a song of praise in the Kyrie part, or gives a prophecy in the Invocation part, he will be corrected either by the pastor, or by an elder, or, if he persists, by the immediate and spontaneous singing of the whole congregation. Most Pentecostals are not aware of the liturgical function of these choruses, yet they are clearly observable. The Pentecostals thus demonstrate that the alternative to a written liturgy is not chaos, but a flexible oral tradition, which allows for variations within the framework of the whole liturgical structure, similar to the possibilities in a jam session of jazz musicians.[22]

As both Hollenweger and other scholars of Pentecostal worship – perhaps most notably Daniel Albrecht[23] – have shown, Pentecostal celebration is in fact considerably more ordered than may at first be imagined. And such patterns do oftentimes fall closely in line with the classical fourfold shape of worship in other Christian traditions, even though neither that nor any other shape is scripted on paper. Yet it is the unscripted nature of Pentecostalism that has perhaps meant that the Pentecostal/charismatic stream of Christianity has been one which was, until relatively recently, excluded from most liturgical study. (The mistaken assumption that the style has no patterns is undoubtedly also a factor.)[24] However, the emphasis on improvisation in Pentecostal and charismatic worship is highly amenable to contemporary liturgical emphasis on a common core with freedom for great flexibility. Particularly where a common core of a tradition is identified, as in Anglicanism, above, elements of Pentecostal style have often been welcomed into the liturgical repertoire of mainstream traditions.[25]

Alternative Worship

Alternative worship has been part of the life of many British churches since the 1980s. It often both appropriates aspects of the seeker-service critique of received liturgy, and yet opts for more participatory forms in an effort to remedy what it perceives as problems with inherited patterns. Indeed, it often draws on longstanding and traditional forms of worship, though tends to do so in a somewhat eclectic, ad hoc way. Not unlike charismatic worship, alternative worship is often characterized by a sense of creative play.

One of its defining marks is that it is often highly technological, drawing on a range of multimedia. Jonny Baker, Doug Gay and Jenny Brown's book on alternative worship – the first of its kind in Britian – uses the analogy of sampling pioneered by pop musicians such as Depeche Mode to describe the kind of approach to tradition often employed in alternative worship:

> The interest in tradition was one of the factors in alt. worship being labelled 'post-modern', because of the way it combines use of advanced mixed-media technology and techniques with an eclectic use of the worship traditions of the church. One way of understanding this is through the metaphor of 'sampling' from music technology. In sampling, a slice of music is extracted from its original setting (whether a break beat from a James Brown song to a moment of the Hallelujah Chorus) and inserted into a new music context, where it combines with other elements to form a new whole.[26]

Baker *et al.* go on to note that something analogous to sampling goes on each time traditions revise their resources for prayer. They too approach what has been inherited selectively. Yet what is distinctive about alternative worship is the way in which fragments of liturgical tradition – rituals, icons, chants, prayers, responses – are inserted into a mixed-media context. The juxtapositions have felt more radical because they have not simply been textual revisions of the old format, but have set up new links between liturgy and contemporary media.[27]

Here are two examples of the kind of ideas developed in alternative worship:

Nails in Wood

Items needed

A large piece of wood – ideally driftwood or something similar – hammers, large nails.

Instructions for setting up

Place some nails and a few hammers on the ground next to the piece of wood.

Description

As an act of confession invite people to come and hammer a nail into the wood. During the confession play or sing a lament. The track 'Protection' by Massive Attack (try the Brian Eno mix) which contains the line 'Protection – you took the force of the blow' is a stunning track to play.

Other ideas

You could give people a nail to take away with them as a reminder.

Frozen

Items needed

A large block of ice (try finding a shop that sells ice for ice sculpture), some scaffolding and chain to suspend the ice from, night lights, small spot lights.

Instructions for setting up

This ritual requires a bit of extra effort to set up but is well worth it. Suspend the ice off the ground with some chains off a scaffolding pole. Project some lights on to it. You'll also need to put a plastic sheet underneath to protect the floor.

Description

Invite people to come and light a night light and place it under the ice to contribute to its melting. This ritual could be part of some intercessions asking God to melt the cold hearts of leaders in situations of oppression or injustice. Or it could be a response asking God to melt the coldness of our own hearts.

Other ideas

A good addition is to record a dripping tap and play it quietly in the background. This also lends itself to some great images of water and ice. Get a video camera and video the ice melting and use that in future services.[28]

It can be noted that each of these examples is amenable to use within the fourfold flow of classical patterns of Christian worship. Each of these examples might, on different occasions, form powerful 'responses' to the word, and yield potential as 'opportunities of transformation'.

'Apt Liturgy'

The symbolism which is so important to alternative worship is also central to another kind of 'non-traditional' worship to receive attention in recent literature, although it – like alternative worship – is not yet a major focus of liturgical theology. In her recent books *Beyond the Good Samaritan* and *Journeying out*, the missiologist Ann Morisy coins the phrase 'apt liturgy' to refer to opportunities outside public worship in which ministers and others 'seize the moment' of pastoral encounter to refer people to the divine in simple, extemporized liturgical forms.

> Apt liturgy is short and simple, and often can take place in mundane environments. Apt liturgy does not require people to cross the threshold of the church . . . apt liturgy is specifically about accessibility and (usually) engaging with people who are having to deal with hard emotions.

By way of example, she continues:

> The first instance of apt liturgy that I encountered took place in a minibus. Members of the Seniors' Club had planned a summer trip to revisit the places to which they had been evacuated during the war. The minister recognized that this provided an opportunity to offer high symbols that could engage with their experience, which no doubt would be characterized by all kinds of complex emotions: gratitude for today being able to live in peace and not war; revitalized by happy memories but disappointed by a community that that no longer expressed the solidarity born of struggle; saddened by the loss of loved ones yet gratified that the family had held together through thick and thin; troubled by a world that despite the optimism at the end of the war didn't seem to have got any better. The minister having recognized the possible range of emotions then had to rise to the challenge of encompassing such diverse and potent emotions in less than eight minutes.[29]

On the one hand, Morisy's use of the term 'liturgy' to describe such an act is somewhat confusing. The kind of spontaneous event to which she refers by this term is 'not to be confused with worship', but is rather more about the whetting appetite for liturgy, nurturing a capacity for the kind of celebration which is consciously organized around scripture and sacrament, for instance. Apt liturgy is, Morisy suggests, 'for those who only half believe or have inchoate beliefs, but recognize their need for reassurance, encouragement and courage'. It concentrates on achieving:

> memories of the heart, i.e. ideas and images that can be pondered; enabling people to cope, especially when they are close to being overwhelmed by emotion; providing symbols or codes that 'waft us heavenward'[30]

in such a way as to resonate with people's human struggles at particular moments. In doing so, it may prepare people at some later stage to enter an explicit domain of belief such as that provided by public worship.

On the other hand, apt liturgy as Morisy understands it may often respond to, or indeed effect, the sense of gathering that is crucial to liturgy, and in its use of symbols may employ established liturgical dynamics to awaken the sense of divine presence in human struggle and to orient inchoate faith towards its ordering and expression in liturgy as more usually understood.

Feminist Liturgies

A key challenge to contemporary liturgical study is that posed by feminist analysis and engagement in liturgical traditions. One issue of major importance is that of 'expansive language', which has a number of dimensions, as Marjorie Procter-Smith outlines:

> Non-sexist language seeks to avoid gender-specific terms. Inclusive language seeks to balance gender references. Emancipatory language seeks to transform language use and to challenge stereotypical gender references.
>
> Non-sexist language suggests that God does not regard our gender,

or that our gender is not relevant to our relationship with God. Inclusive language implies that God does not regard our gender, but that both women and men possess equal status before God. Emancipatory language assumes that God is engaged in women's struggles for emancipation, even to the point of identifying with those who struggle . . .

Emancipatory language must make women visible.[31]

Feminist critique of inherited traditions of worship has demanded that male-dominated language in liturgy if not expunged should be expanded to include a range of complementary feminine metaphors, as well as those inspired by the non-human creation. Hence, the efforts of feminist Christians have enabled considerable change to liturgical language about both humankind and the divine. The official liturgies of the churches are increasingly sensitive to the issues: a number of translations of the scriptures are now available in which reference to the human race in general and to the Christian people in particular are rendered in contemporary idioms that include both genders (so 'man' becomes 'humanity', 'brothers' becomes 'brothers and sisters', etc.). Language about God has been more controversial: a number of feminist collections of prayers now freely name God 'mother' and in terms of a range of other female images. Janet Morley's *All Desires Known*[32] and Nicola Slee's *Praying like a Woman* are examples of the genre at its best. Ascriptions such as 'mother' have, however, rarely found their way into the denominational prayerbooks.[33] Except in specifically feminist collections, female language is by no means used to such an extent that it balances male and female metaphors. One of the key tasks for feminist interpreters of scripture has been, in the title of Ann Loades' book, which is itself a scriptural image (Luke 15.8–10), to go *Searching for Lost Coins*[34] and so recover female images which have been obscured, sidelined or otherwise fallen out of use; and then to put them to use in worship.

Trinitarian language has also proved difficult to re-envision and revise at an official level: the phrase 'creator, redeemer, sustainer' as an alternative to 'Father, Son, Spirit' for a short time enjoyed widespread use. However, it has come to be roundly regarded as inadequate for its modalist connotations, in which the personal dimension of the traditional idiom may be diminished or lost. Recently, though, the phrase 'holy eternal Majesty, holy incarnate

Word, holy abiding Spirit' has found some usage in official denominational resources,[35] and it is possible to imagine use of such a formula at least as an additional enrichment, if not as a replacement, to 'Father, Son, Spirit' in the likes of benedictions and baptismal formulae.

One notable resource on expansive language in relation to use of scripture in public worship is the three-volume *Readings for the Assembly*,[36] which casts the lectionary readings of the Revised Common Lectionary for the Sunday cycles of years A, B and C in more inclusive mode. In this resource 'LORD/Lord' is often rendered 'Living One', 'kingdom' becomes 'dominion', and by these and similar amendments, exclusive language is unobtrusively edged out in favour of terms which in any case can do equal or better justice to the original and root meanings of the words of scripture. This important resource was compiled by Gail Ramshaw and Gordon Lathrop who were together also responsible for one of the most striking seasonal examples of expansive language in their prayers for Easter published as part of their meditative collection *Easter: A Sourcebook*.[37] These prayers – one for each of the seven Sundays of the Easter season, which runs between and includes both Easter Sunday and Pentecost Sunday – employ no fewer than 21 fresh metaphors for God, each of which is drawn from scripture itself: the metaphors of light, beauty, rest, bread, milk, honey, shepherd, gate, lamb, grove, lover, well, sovereign, banquet, crown, holy one, altar and cloud are employed, as in 'O God, our light, our beauty, our rest' for which Psalm 27.11, Psalm 27.4, and Matthew 11.29 are cited as sources of the images. As with this example, a chapter and verse reference is offered for each of these diverse images of God.

Nicola Slee's poem 'Litany to a Dark God' provides another example of how expansive language traces its roots to scripture. This poem is a meditation upon Song of Songs 1.5–6:

> I hear her voice in the night shadows
> but I do not see her face
> I feel her breath on the cold night air
> but I cannot touch her flesh
> near to me as breathing
> intimate as touching

in the darkness she eludes my grasp
she evades my touch
all her ways are strange to me
and all her paths are hidden

She is speaking to me in the darkness
but I do not comprehend what she is saying
She is leading me in the darkness
but I cannot tell where she is moving
She is pursuing me in the darkness
but I cannot discover her purpose
Under the velvet cover of night she seduces me
and I cannot resist her advances
Under the blanket of stars she gazes at me
and I cannot refuse her glances
Drawn to her darkness
I come in under the belly of her shadow
Entranced by her obscurity
I enter in where knowledge is no more

Here I must stay under the dark gaze of her loving
Here I must rest under the fragrance of her silence
Here I must wait under the shadow of her wooing
while she speaks to me
and she sings to me
and she cradles me
and croons to me
in words no other may utter
in a language unknown to any other lover

And she will charm me and bind me
She will pierce me and bless me
She will fill me and empty me
She will rouse me and quiet me
She will wound me and heal me

She will quicken me and deaden me
in her deep and unyielding darkness
which no tongue may name nor finger trace
no searching plumb nor mind guess

And I will enter into this darkness
where I have never walked before
And I will submit into this darkness
to a terror never dared before
And I will yield to this darkness
to a loving never ventured before

And of her darkness I must know and I must know nothing
And in this darkness I must be made and I must be unmade
And of her darkness I must be possessed and dispossessed of all
things[38]

Feminist liturgical consciousness is not only concerned with language, however. A notable early collection of early feminist worship resources, Rosemary Radford Ruether's *Woman-Church* imaged the feminist Christian assembly gathering in a 'celebration centre' in which the 'conversation circle' was a primary spatial arrangement,[39] an antidote to hierarchical arrangements of space. And Janet Walton sketches the impact of feminist sensitivity on the gesture and ceremonial that may or may not be employed:

Horizontal gestures prevail in feminist liturgies; they suggest equality and interdependence; they affirm God known among us. Generally we do not look up to find God. We connect with each other to give and receive blessings.

We pray with our eyes open and without bowing our heads. Not that we do not acknowledge God's authority, but we know God does not require bowing our heads and closing our eyes. Bowing our heads for a blessing, as Marjorie Proctor-Smith points out, is 'a non-reciprocal action' related to experiences that remind us of a male domination. It signals an inferior social status that has not promoted women's well-being. Closing one's eyes is dangerous in an unjust society. Though we presume we are safe in our gatherings, we do not repeat actions that have historically limited, demeaned or hurt us.

Kneeling poses problems, too. We recognize its value to remind us of reverence for God and one another, but when women kneel to receive Communion or a blessing from men, rather than promoting an experience of reverence, it can be a reminder of sexual violation or subservience. Since women are frequently victims of violence at the hands of men, we practice standing and sitting rather than kneeling. We want to remind ourselves every time we can that sexual violence is rooted in misplaced power, that is, when anyone presumes power over another. Feminist liturgies intend to provide occasions to practice gestures of resistance and expressions of shared power.[40]

Feminist liturgical perspectives therefore offer a range of major challenges and contributions to the future of Christian worship.

Postcolonial Perspectives

If feminist theology poses an inescapable range of challenges for contemporary Christian worship, another major challenger is postcolonial theology, with which liturgical studies has as yet made very little engagement.[41] Postcolonial theology is concerned to critique and confront the domination of European modes of thought and to reverse both the subjugation of Black nations in the era of 'empire' and its continuing legacy. Postcolonial theology seeks to develop 'a new mode of imagining, a new cultural logic, posited over against the Eurocentric monologic and the colonial manner of thinking and visioning reality'.[42] If feminist theology, among other things 'searches for lost coins' in the Christian tradition in order to enable different readings of it, perhaps somewhat similarly postcolonial theology looks for 'openings for oppositional readings, uncovers suppressed voices and, more pertinently, has as its foremost concern victims and their plight'.[43]

Postcolonial engagement with inherited liturgical resources will in time develop a comprehensive agenda, although given that 'racism is perpetuated when the colour black is used in negative, and white in positive, ways',[44] one of the first and most pressing arguments it might pick with liturgical traditions is with the almost consistent identifications between light and goodness, and darkness and evil, employed in so many modes of prayer. The liturgical problem is closely related to issues in biblical interpretation, for the alliances are in part rooted in scripture: apparently 'God is light and in him there is no darkness at all' (1 John 1.9). Oppositional readings of scripture might, then, involve painstaking readings of biblical references to colour in order to establish that there is in fact a more varied range of alliance than might be imagined from most liturgical use: white is the colour of skin disease, for starters (Exod. 4.6; Num. 12.10 etc.). However, it will do more: a postcolonial reading of scripture will offer a defiant challenge to Eurocentric thinking that perpetuates such alliances between darkness and black, and light and white. These may find their roots in a tradition of interpretation that stretches back to patristic origins but it certainly cannot always be located in the Bible itself: '[a]mong patristic writers, darkness became a major theme for discussing the presence of sin. Light came to the Gentiles once they turned from their life of sin.'[45] Thus, blackness in early Christian thought overwhelmingly conveyed social values and a moral rank subordinate to whiteness, an attitude that became a cornerstone of western cultural views reinforced by the slave trade, economics, Egyptology, physical and social sciences, and later Christendom.[46]

Denominational liturgical resources by and large have yet to address the challenge of reworking light and darkness imagery, and if and when they do the task will be enormous because the worship resources of many European churches are unconscientized to the difficulties of such imagery. As just one example, the Church of England's *Common Worship* resource for daily prayer makes much use of the imagery, indeed accentuating it throughout the Christmas cycle of seasons from Advent through to Candlemas. And *Common Worship* is just one of many contemporary resources that has recently revived the ancient office of the Lucernarium – lamplighting – for which a plethora of new prayers have also recently been written. Engaging with postcolonial perspectives will, however, mean considering rewording prayers and finding alternative metaphors to avoid that which is potentially offensive, reinforces stereotypes, bolsters systems of inequality and colludes with subordination and prejudice. It is not yet clear how this might be done, although as a modest positive suggestion, perhaps some of the difficulties might be minimized by replacing the language of light with that of 'radiance' or 'brightness'. Detached from the language of light, 'bright' and 'radiant' imply no particular colour, avoiding dehumanizing associations. Likewise, the language of darkness might be replaced by the more neutral notion of 'shadows'. Again, this implies no particular colour.

Another intriguing potential way forward in continued use of light and darkness imagery – albeit best contained within a more expansive reper-toire – emerges in the recent liturgical provisions for the Anglican Church of Kenya. *Our Modern Services* is replete with imagery of light and darkness, and it must be said that it is not always possible to imagine how it could escape the kind of critique to which postcolonial critics subject appropriation of such imagery from scriptural sources. However, in commentary about how the language of light is used in the book, it is at least sometimes configured above all with 'weight' as this contributes to the meaning of 'glory', rather than with 'darkness' as an a symbol of blindness, lostness or sin. For example, the confession used in morning and evening prayer reads in part:

> We have done wrong and neglected to do right;
> our sins weigh heavily on our hearts;
> Lord, have mercy, count them not against us.
> Grant us the joy of forgiveness
> and lighten our hearts with the glory of Christ,
> who died and rose again for us.[47]

About this prayer, the authors comment:

> The heart of the confession is a play on the Hebrew word for 'glory' (*kabod*) which originally designated 'weight', 'substance', or what could be called 'gravitas' and developed, according to George Caird, under the influence of Ezekiel, into 'brightness' or 'radiance'. Therefore sins 'weigh heavily …' and there is a plea: 'lighten our hearts with the glory of Christ'. 'Lighten' covers the meanings of 'make less heavy' and also of 'brighten'. 'Glory' carries the meanings of 'weight' and of 'radiance'. The irony of praying for our hearts 'to be made less heavy by something which is heavy' is probably

missed by most people, but was deliberate. The themes of 'heart' and 'lighten' also echo Matthew 11.29–30: 'Take my yoke upon you, and learn from me; for I am gentle and lowly in heart, and you find rest for your souls. For my yoke is easy, and my burden is light'.[48]

This Kenyan confession is perhaps an example of the potential for reconfiguration of familiar imagery drawing on alternative yet deeply embedded scriptural allusions.

Gay and Lesbian Worshipping Communities

Oppositional readings in postcolonial theology also relate to the purposeful determination to 'queer' Christian traditions in gay and lesbian theology. 'Queer' is the preferred designation of many gay and lesbian theologians,[49] for dictionary definitions suggest that to queer means to spoil, disrupt, or put in a bad light. 'Queer' is, then, a conscious and deliberate to challenge the tradition.

Elizabeth Stuart's writing on the liturgy from her lesbian feminist perspective is one of the most articulate attempts to offer a 'queer' reading of the Christian liturgical tradition and to assert that the tradition itself has great potential to queer socially constructed roles, gender, sexuality, race and class 'in such a way to point to their non-ultimacy', which is of liberative significance for those who are marginalized because of others' perceptions of them. In relation to feminism, she writes:

> The mysterious energy that flows over us [in the liturgy] sends us to live out our culturally-negotiated identities differently, to parody them in order to better witness to the new creation being born in us. We live as people of a new reality, a reality that is mysteriously present to us in the liturgy and in particular in Eucharist. In the liturgy, then, women enter into a magical realm, the space of between, the space of the dawn, the womb of creation, a space in which feminism reaches its fulfillment in the eschatological erasure of maleness and femaleness. It is the place in which queer theory conquers its own nihilism because here is its point

and guarentee, participation in the divine life. It is a space in which the material orders are transfigured and become windows into a different type of living. It is the space of heaven, of life beyond the power of death and life beyond the power of rationalism. In this space gender is dissolved, time is absorbed into reality, miracles happen – bread and wine are transubstantiated, angels and the whole company of heaven including the dead are present with the living. In short, the liturgy, particularly the Eucharist, is a space beyond patriarchy although patriarchy has attempted to colonise it and feminism has largely retreated before it.[50]

In this perspective, liturgy mandates and energizes the subversion of established male-centred power.

Lesbian and gay perspectives are increasingly important in debate about worship, because they are now emerging in relation to the recent decisions of some Christian communities to consciously welcome and celebrate the presence of homosexual persons in their assemblies. Liturgies of affirmation are scattered in different places, such as Ann Day's in the ecumenical collection *Touch Holiness*:

Spirit of God, we thank you for all who let the light of love shine forth. And those among us who are your lesbian and gay daughters and sons, O God, are especially grateful for the brave and loving witness of churches now open to affirming of our lives and our gifts. Most particularly at this time, we celebrate this church as it publicly welcomes all who seek to worship and serve Jesus Christ.

Thanks be to you, O God, for that inclusive love which makes our gospel 'good news', our communities true reflections of your reign, and our hearts full of joy and hope.

Even as we rejoice in the light that shines, we remember how much its brightness might be increased. There is so much yet to be done for us and by us:

So much justice to be established, so much pain yet to be healed, so much peace yet to be realized, so much love yet to pour forth . . .[51]

Other liturgical resources are emerging, notably Kittridge Cherry and

Zalmon Sherwood's resource for the Metropolitan Community Church, *Equal Rites*.[52] It remains the case, however, that most official liturgies as yet tend to make little, if any, mention of the 'love that dare not speak its name'. Unsurprisingly, then, Christian worship sometimes takes place in gay and lesbian communities without reference to the liturgical forms of the churches that have excluded them. However, it is notable that these sometimes nevertheless employ deep liturgical dynamics. For example, note the order, the participation, the gestures, and the parallel between the 'greeting portion' and 'the peace' of traditional liturgies in this extract describing the 'Gospel Hour' hosted by Morticia de Ville and the 'Gospel Girls' in a downtown bar in Atlanta, Georgia:

> These services have a form as consistent as any church's 'order of worship'. After her opening numbers Morticia introduces Romona Dugger, the number two Gospel Girl . . . Her songs are emotional and passionate. They are spiritually explicit as well. Ramona . . . is a straight, young African American woman . . . When asked about proselytising during the services, she said:
>
> [. . .] I'm not preaching to anybody. But I do think there are so many people who are hungry to know that God does love them . . . You got to look up and know you are not alone . . .
>
> The most recent Gospel Girl is Alicia Kelly, a young muscular black man . . . She pours a fantastic amount of energy into her dancing, or 'shouting'. The congregation watches her transport herself acrobatically across the stage. She appears possessed by the Holy Ghost . . .
>
> Almost immediately Morticia appears and introduces the 'Greeting Portion' of the service. She invites strangers to go up and introduce themselves to one another. Morticia often leads the way and begins to mingle with the crowd . . . When the service resumes, the energy level increases in anticipation of the 'High Church Sing Along', the highlight of the service. Morticia, Ramona, Alicia, and occasional guests sit on bar stools. They lead the crowd in verses of favourite hymns such as: 'When the Roll is Called Up Yonder', 'Because He Lives, I Can Face Tomorrow', and 'There is Power in the Blood of the Lamb'. The volume and quality of the congregation's singing would be the envy of any church. During these hymns, partici-

pants will occasionally close their eyes, bow their heads, a few others may raise their hands ... Tears are no strangers at these services.

Each Gospel Hour concludes in exactly the same fashion. Perched on bar stools, the Gospel Girls lip-sync a rousing version of 'Looking for a City'. Members of the audience grab cocktail napkins. These are used as hankies which nearly everyone in the room waves back and forth, to and fro, round and round, in time with the music. This waving is not random, but is instead a highly choreographed routine which originated among the congregation itself ... The finale is a Gospel song, 'See You in the Rapture'. It, also, is a high energy piece, with a lot of congregational participation. Often a dozen or more men take the stage and form a chorus line several deep ... It is as highly choreographed as the napkin ritual ... The 'folks in the pews' created these rituals, they own them.

The theology behind the lyrics of 'See You in the Rapture' are explicitly fundamentalist. The style of the dancing, on the other hand, is campy. The emotions underneath are implicitly sexual. It is a fitting conclusion to this ambiguous performance of Gospel in drag.[53]

The Gospel Hour is in a sense a seeker service, especially hospitable to people in a particular culture, and expressing some features of that culture. Yet, as just shown, it also echoes longstanding traditions. As queer Christians become more vocal about their participation in worship, and lesbian and gay majority congregations develop their own forms of liturgy, the queer challenge to dominant culture – forcibly expressed in Elizabeth Stuart's reflections, above – offers a mission perspective from which the whole church can learn.

Children's Liturgies

As we have seen, the desire to include children more fully in worship was a major impetus for New Patterns for Worship and recent liturgical developments in the Church of England. With a number of Protestant traditions, these also include a trend towards what is sometimes called 'sacramental belonging'. This involves children previously excluded from eucharistic sharing now being fully involved in sacramental celebration. In embracing such developments, the Church of England at least has followed the lead of a number of other provinces of the Anglican Communion, who in 1985 collectively recommended that children be admitted to holy communion:

> We wish to affirm on theological grounds that children of all ages are included among those for whom Christ died, that children of all ages are recipients of his love, that children of all ages are equally persons in the people of God, and that children of all ages have an active ministry in Christ among his people and in the world. We see no dogmatic or other credible basis for regarding some who are baptized as eligible to receive communion while others are not. We believe this is to run contrary to the inclusive character of the Gospel . . .[54]

Consequently, children have increasingly been seen as crucial to the renewal of the church and its worship, at least in many places. Churches have, however, struggled with the implications of what children's sacramental belonging may require in terms of change to inherited patterns: welcoming children to the table certainly means more than accommodating them to existing patterns without more wholesale changes, as New Patterns for Worship demonstrated in its major rethinking of how Anglican resources might be presented centrally and then constructed locally. Advocates of liturgical renewal that invites and involves children are, therefore, by no means naive about the cost of such change. David Holeton suggests that the full participation of children in worship will mean nothing less that the 'reconstruction of selves and attitudes':

> Once the right of presence in the eucharistic assembly and, consequently, admission to communion is guaranteed, we need to ask some serious questions about what children will find in the midst of that assembly. It is here that the most serious work will need to be done because this will involve the reconstruction of ourselves and our attitudes towards worship.[55]

Without doubt, this requires considerable vulnerability from the adults responsible for children in the church. The other side of the risk of vulnerability, however, is the strength that may be gained from the endeavour to welcome the young, and it is upon this that Elizabeth Smith concentrates as she identifies some hopes for how the fuller inclusion of children might bring promise to the whole church:

> Renewed worship that happens as a result of children's inclusion will mean some changes in practice. It will also mean a shift in the spiritual orientation of the adult worshippers. Over time, some of the children's naïve confidence will rub off, and it will smooth down some of the adults' doctrinal hackles. Some of the children's hunger for physical connection and bodily movement, for touch and caress, for eye-contact and direct verbal addresses, will rub off, and it will awaken some of the adults' dormant awareness of their own bodies in prayer. Some of the children's questions will stay around, and create a climate in which some of the adults feel free to ask questions too . . .[56]

Certainly, *questions* are key to the gifts that children can offer to Christian assemblies according to Mary Collins. She writes about the way in which liturgy for children should not evade the paschal character of Christian faith – its focus on the death and resurrection of Jesus – however difficult ideas about death and resurrection might be to conceive intellectually and, especially in relation to the suffering of the cross, face emotionally. As Collins elaborates, children's capacity to imagine and fantasize is a test for their adult companions in Christian worship, because in so far as children often easily find themselves able to believe in what Tolkien called 'euchatastrophes' – 'stories with happy endings' – the presence of children in the assembly invites the whole church to reflect upon the depth of its sense that the paschal mystery of death and resurrection is a dependable lens on the world and its ultimate future. Children challenge the church to consider if and how they believe that 'the Gospel is . . . the ultimate "euchatastrophe", the final fulfillment of all human fantasies about a world where things turn out right':

> The presence of children in the Christian community confronts all of us with a choice. It forces us to decide whether the fantasy of the Gospel is true and worthy of a lifetime's devotion and love, or whether it is false, another

in a series of illusions about a world doomed to inglorious extinction at the hands of stupidly realistic men. If the child is right, then the world has a future and so do we. If the child is wrong, then we should 'all fold our hands and wait for the end with stoic composure'.[57]

Children, then, may lead the church to the heart of faith, and of course they may teach childlike ways to believe it. 'The mystery proclaimed in Jesus is that the forces of diminishment and destruction are real indeed, but the power and purpose of God will ultimately prevail',[58] and this conviction is key to what Christian worship celebrates, to what in the end makes Christian worship distinct from the vacuousness of much 'celebration' in contemporary culture, which is the focus of Paul Pruyser's critique cited above.

Conclusion: Unity in Diversity

In this chapter, we have traversed a very broad range of perspectives that contribute to the richness of the current diversity of Christian worship. Different styles have substance: they demand that contemporary convergence about Christian worship, such as that around the emphasis on the basic shape of the liturgy which we considered in Chapter 1, is thought about in more inclusive ways. On the one hand, this will mean no less than that marginal forms of worship are recognized as sometimes sharing at least some of the dynamics of mainstream patterns, just as we saw in our example from Pentecostal worship, in which classical components of worship, such as kyries, found closely related expressions, and in our attention to worship in a gay and lesbian community, in which the 'greeting portion' mirrored the 'greeting of peace' in traditional liturgical forms. At the same time, we have considered so-called alternative worship, which consciously employs fragments of liturgical tradition, but without as yet often having been so concerned with developing a clear sense of the deep structures of the liturgy such as has happened, for example, in *New Patterns for Worship* as it has clarified a basic framework for its diverse 'directory' of resources, not least as a means of including children in worship that remains strongly informed by the 'core' of a tradition.

On the other hand, some of the perspectives we have considered represent nothing less than very sizable challenges both to the weight of inherited liturgical tradition and to the otherwise good gains of contemporary ecumenical convergence concerning the liturgy. Elaborating on points made in the introductory chapter, we have seen in this present chapter some ways in which those informed by feminist sensitivities might 'pray between the lines' of denominational liturgies, with examples of expansive language clearly suggesting alternatives to official texts that may be experienced as intolerably oppressive in their limited repertoire of images for both the divine and humankind. And we have also considered some aspects of the argument with liturgical texts and practices that is emerging from postcolonial perspectives.

Clearly, it is not only 'apt liturgy', in the sense intended by Ann Morisy, that is deeply related to questions about mission, about how the church tells the truth about both the human condition and the availability of grace, and invites participation in ways that can be seen, heard and experienced as attractive enough to merit attention. The kinds of new issues and fresh expressions of Christian worship we have considered in this chapter are all – though perhaps to greater or lesser extent – likely to have relevance in very many congregations. It is naive to think, though, that the tensions they represent are easily reconcilable, especially when they are held in the wider context of the other important issues addressed throughout the previous chapters of this book. This notwithstanding, a concern for human flourishing requires awareness of the diverse issues that this chapter has touched upon, and presiders at least will most certainly need to be sensitive to them if they are to foster the kind of inclusivity that embraces all God's people. Each of the challenges might be addressed with the conviction that 'a community that faithfully attends to the narratives of the crucified Jesus cannot be a community that excludes'.[59] Yet while all these very different ways of worship are ones which are likely to stretch and challenge, we may also hope that

a deepening sense of 'being church' is . . . part of the unexpected side of the work of inclusion. The movement from adopting an 'inclusive' attitude on the part of the leadership to the actual life of being a place of 'belonging' is itself a maturation, both theological and moral. This, I contend, is part of what it means to be a faithful people of God in the world, to 'grow up in every way' into Christ (Ephesians 4.15). Participating in the movement from inclusivity to the spirituality of belonging to one another is an image of the Christian life itself.[60]

Further Reading

Daniel Albrecht, *Rites in the Spirit: A Ritual Approach to Pentecostal and Charismatic Worship* (Sheffield: Sheffield Academic Press, 1999).

Thomas F. Best and Dagmar Heller (eds), *Worship Today: Understanding, Practice, Ecumenical Implications* (Geneva: WCC Publications, 2004).

Ronald P. Byars, *The Future of Protestant Worship: Beyond the Worship Wars* (Lousiville, KY: Westminster John Knox Press, 2002).

Marva Dawn, *A Royal Waste of Time: The Splendor of Worshiping God and Being Church for the World* (Grand Rapids, MI: Eerdmans, 1999).

Marva Dawn, *Reaching out Without Dumbing down: A Theology of Worship for this Urgent Time* (Grand Rapids, MI: Eerdmans, 1995).

Christopher Ellis, *Gathering: A Theology and Spirituality of Worship in the Free Church Tradition* (London: SCM Press, 2004).

Thomas G. Long, *Beyond the Worship Wars: Building Vital and Faithful Worship* (New York: Alban Institute, 2001).

Ruth A. Meyers (ed.), *Children at the Table: Essays on Children and the Eucharist* (New York: Church Publishing, 1994).

Marjorie Procter-Smith, *In Her Own Rite: Constructing Feminist Liturgical Tradition* (Akron, OH: Order of St Luke, 2000).

Gail Ramshaw, *Under the Tree of Life: The Religion of a Feminist Christian* (New York: Continuum, 1998).

Frank Senn, *The Witness of the Worshiping Community: Liturgy and the Practice of Evangelism* (New York: Paulist Press, 1993).

James White, *Protestant Worship: Traditions in Transition* (Louisville, KY: Westminster John Knox Press, 1989).

6

Cycles and Crises: Time for Worship

What are the rhythms of Christian liturgy?
On what life-events does liturgy focus?
Might the Good Friday reproaches be seen as a reversal of eucharistic prayer?
How does baptismal spirituality undergird Christian ministries?

In this chapter we explore various ways in which Christian worship relates to time: the day, week, season, year, and human life-cycle. In the earlier parts of the chapter, we focus in turn on Sunday and then two of the major cycles of the liturgical year. We then move on to consider the human life-cycle, and the chapter concludes with a particular focus on baptism. Each is in a way related to mission, as Christian worship addresses a range of human needs and the various seasons of human living.

The Past and Future of Sunday

From a very early period of the life of the church, Sunday has been the primary time of Christian worship, and it remains so today. Mark Searle points to the core meaning of Sunday when he suggests that it is 'essentially a post-resurrection appearance of the Risen Christ'. Sunday is most obviously associated with the resurrection of Jesus, which according to each of the four

Gospel evangelists occurred on 'the first day of the week' (Matt. 28.1; Mark 16.1–2; Luke 24.1; John 20.1).

In the Acts, we find Paul sharing the word and breaking bread on the first day of the week (Acts 20.7–11) and in the Corinthian correspondence he seems to attach particular significance to the first day as one for attending to Christian duty (1 Cor. 16.2). Until AD 321, worship on Sunday would most likely have taken place either early in the morning or late in the evening, before or after work, on what was an ordinary working day. From 321, when the Roman state designated Sunday as one for rest and Christian worship, different practical arrangements became possible.

Theologically, the first day also quickly became known as 'the Lord's day' (e.g. Rev. 1.10), presumably in honour of Christ's resurrection: the earliest post-biblical document of the Christian tradition, the *Didache*, refers to 'the Lord's day – his special day' when Christians are to 'come together to break bread and give thanks first confessing your sins so that your sacrifice may be pure' (*Didache* 14). And it seems that the resurrection was quickly regarded as transcending time, with Sunday also labelled 'the eighth day' of divine recreation. So, for example, the Letter of Barnabas, sometimes dated to c. AD 80, includes this designation, while at the same time conveying some of the felt-tension in the early Christian community about the adequacy of the inherited category of 'sabbath' as a lens on their special day of worship:

> [Jesus said:] 'It is not the Sabbaths now celebrated that please me, but the Sabbath which I made, and on which, on bringing all things to their rest, I will begin an eighth day, that is a new world'. That is why we celebrate as a joyous feast the eighth day on which Jesus rose from the dead and, after appearing to his disciples, ascended into heaven.[1]

The note of joy in Barnabas' letter seems characteristic of the tone of extant testimony to early Christian celebration on the day 'on which Jesus rose from the dead'. Moreover, 'resurrection' means, literally, 'stand up', and for their prayer, it seems that many Christians typically adopted the posture of standing, the gesture itself a sign of Christ's victory.

Barnabas' engagement with the notion of sabbath points to the way in which the Christian Sunday was both related to and distinct from inherited

Jewish tradition. At first, Sunday emerged as a day of worship alongside the sabbath and worship in the temple. Over time, however, the greater parting of the ways between the Christian movement and its Jewish antecedents meant that sabbath worship was abandoned, and some of its themes were transferred to Sunday. Barnabas echoes one of the Hebrew scriptures' understandings of sabbath as a day of rest, the crown of God's creation (Exod. 20.8–11; Gen. 1.3–5). However, another tradition is also present in the Hebrew Bible, centred not on the divine work of creation but rather on the stories of divine liberation of the children of Israel from their captivity in Egypt (Deut. 5.12–15). The Deuteronomic emphasis on liberation from bondage provided a type for understanding the resurrection of Christ as God's new act of freedom, and both traditions combine in the sense that while 'slaves cannot take a day off; free people can'.[2]

Although the place of Sunday is assured as the key occasion for worship in the Christian tradition, it should be noted that at the present time it is at least to some measure being renegotiated in the face of contemporary western cultural shifts. It is undoubtedly the case that Sunday congregations have declined in cultural contexts in which worship now competes with a wide variety of leisure activities – sports, shopping and DIY, etc. – which have emerged as evermore popular Sunday past-times. In this situation, many congregations are beginning to offer opportunity for worship at other times in the week, and the Church of England report *Mission-Shaped Church* among other things charts the rise of congregations gathering at other times. Among the possibilities discussed in *Mission-Shaped Church* are midweek congregations arising out of Alpha or other evangelistic groups, held on the regular evening of the original evangelistic event and 'closer to Alpha in style and feel' than a 'traditional Sunday service',[3] and services held in church schools midweek at the end of the school day, accessible to both pupils and their family circles.[4] How these alternatives to Sunday worship may develop remains to be seen, yet for the time being it remains the case that the fact Sunday has held particular meaning for Christians shows Christianity, like its Jewish antecedent, to be a faith that is deeply concerned with time. The same concern is also apparent in the Christian celebration of seasons of the year.

Perspectives on Lent and Easter

The great hymn, the Exsultet, is sung in the Roman Catholic and some other traditions during the lighting of the paschal candle from the new fire each year at the Easter Vigil. The hymn asks that the candlelight before the community 'mingle[s] with the lights of heaven', confident that 'this is the night truly blessed when heaven is wedded to earth and we are reconciled with God'.[5] The phrase 'this is the night' is repeated through the hymn, and is reminiscent of the questions that children ask as part of the celebration of the Jewish Passover, 'why is this night not like any other night?' And this echo of the Passover is in fact a clue to the origins of the Christian celebration of Easter, which developed out of a Christian twist on the theme of Passover. The night of the Easter Vigil is by implication 'not like any other', as climactic and defining for Christians as Passover is for Jews.

And so, just as the week has its nodal point in Sunday, so the year has its climax in Easter, which is sometimes referred to as 'the great Sunday', just as Sunday is sometimes called 'a little Easter'. These overlapping terms point to the common core meaning of both Sunday and Easter as celebrations of the resurrection. However, the historical development of a stress on resurrection at Easter was by no means simple, and such an Easter emphasis in fact developed out of a more complex annual focus on the new life of Jesus only as this was linked with an equally emphatic stress on his passion and suffering. A major insight into the early development of Easter is to be found in the alternative terminology still used for the festival in a number of European languages – for whereas the word 'Easter' comes from the old English word *eastre* (a spring festival of pagan origin), romance languages continue to use the term 'pasch' to name the celebration. The ongoing use of pasch in some languages has continuity with the focus of early Christian celebration which emphasized the passion and suffering (*paschien* = to suffer) of Jesus, as a kind of 'Christian Passover'. Our link with the early church would be better reflected in English language if 'Easter' were also to be substituted with another phrase related to the semantics of 'pasch'.

An emphasis on the suffering and resurrection of Jesus as a kind of Christian Passover is itself embedded in the New Testament. For example, it is found in Paul's call to the Corinthians to 'celebrate the festival' 'because our paschal lamb, Christ, has been sacrificed for us' (1 Cor. 5.7–8). Here he employs the Old Testament stories of exodus, which the Passover recalls, with the cross and the resurrection of Jesus understood through the interpretive lens of the memory of the Hebrews' exodus. Reflecting the early stress on both suffering and resurrection considered together, the classical Christian Triduum (three days) celebrations from Maundy Thursday evening through to Easter Sunday were at first considered (and are perhaps still best considered) as a single liturgical event marking the 'passing over' of Christ from death to new life. Only at a later stage in the church's liturgical developments did these days come to be regarded as a series of separate though related events.

One of the ways that the Old Testament exodus traditions gave shape to emerging Christian understanding can be seen in the way that the early church adopted from Jewish understanding a concept of active remembrance which is central to the Passover. The following words from the Mishnah tractate Pesachim, a Jewish commentary on the Torah (and particularly its story of exodus) give a sense of the key idea:

> In every generation individuals are obliged to regard themselves as if they themselves were brought out from Egypt; for it is said, 'Because of this, what Yahweh did for me when I left Egypt' (Ex. 13.8). Therefore, we are obliged to give thanks, to offer praise . . . and to hymn the one who has done for our fathers and for us all these wonders, who has led us out of slavery and into freedom, out of sorrow to joy, out of mourning to a day of festival, out of darkness to great light, and out of subjugation to redemption.[6]

The tract indicates that the Passover was understood to involve a making present of the ancient liberation – what was done for 'our fathers' was also done 'for us', and so comes the obligation to give thanks and praise. One of the places where this understanding carries over into Christian understanding is in the eucharist, with the 'last supper' broadly set in the context of Passover, with eucharistic anamnesis attracting the kind of interpretation present in the Pesachim: what was done in the event of the last supper, and in the cross which the supper is widely understood to prefigure, was done 'for us', ancient and contemporary.

Although great clarity about how the Christian pasch emerged is now impossible, it is at least clear that by some means it became the earliest annual celebration of the church (possibly in Jerusalem c.135 and Rome c. AD 165), and that it continued to develop over a period of time. Many of the details of the early paschal celebrations are, however, somewhat vague. This is due in no small part to the conflicting biblical chronologies of the date of Jesus' death – there is disagreement between the Gospel writers about the night of the supper and whether it related to the Jewish Passover, and so took place on either Nissan 14 or 15 in the Jewish calendar: Mark 14.14; Luke 22.8, 15; John 19.32–36 are the root cause of the confusion. The disagreement about the date of the supper, and therefore Jesus' death the following day, is reflected in a fascinating exchange of letters in the second century, involving the 'Quartodecimens' who argued for the linking of Easter to Nissan 14, and others, who opposed them. Their opposition was related in part to the prior development of Sunday as the principal day of Christian worship, for they argued that the Christian Passover ought to culminate on a Sunday, whereas the Quartodecimens by fixing the celebration to the Jewish calendar date of Nissan 14 preferred to allow the possibility of a midweek celebration. Perhaps because Christian Sunday worship was already well-established, the arguments of the Quartodecimens' opponents won out in the fourth-century settlement to celebrate the resurrection on a 'great Sunday' of the year.

It seems that Lent developed at first separately to the celebrations of pasch, principally as a concentrated time of preparation for initiation by baptism. The idea of developing a 40-day programme of catechesis for baptism may have grown out of church practice first of all known in Alexandria, Eygpt. Before long, this was linked imaginatively to Jesus' post-baptismal period in the wilderness (Mark 1.9–13 and parallels). But where the Gospels present Jesus in a sequence from baptism to ascesis, Lent developed a pattern of ascesis followed by baptism: Lent was used as a time *leading* to baptism.

Over time, Lent and Easter may have become fused as a resurrection emphasis for Easter developed universally in replacement of the earlier 'Passover' emphasis. Perhaps this provoked a connection with scriptural material on baptism as immersion in Christ's death and resurrection (as in Rom. 6.1–14). In any case, however misty the origins of Lent and Easter may be in the period before the fourth century, it is clear that very quickly after the Council of Nicaea, a standardization was achieved, with a 40-day period prefixed to Easter, concentrated on welcoming, teaching and sharing sacramentally with new believers. Indeed, it seems that in at least some places in the fourth century, Easter was regarded as the only appropriate time for Christian baptism, while other places allowed some other occasions, particularly Pentecost. Nevertheless, it seems that, for many, baptism did not happen randomly but rather found its meaning in the context of the seasons and their respective emphases.

One of the key sources for understanding the development of liturgy for the periods within Lent and Easter is the witness of a fourth-century Spanish nun called Egeria. She is significant not least because she is one of very few early female writers about Christian worship whose work has been preserved.[7]

Egeria kept a journal of her experience in Jerusalem in what she refers to as 'the Great Week' (Holy Week) sometime in the 380s, when she attended the liturgies of these days. Her witness allows us to see that by the 380s the earlier emphasis on the pasch as a single liturgical celebration had become fragmented into a number of foci, and she offers fascinating insight into the way in which a sense of the historical sequence of the events of Jesus' final days before crucifixion were dramatized in liturgical celebrations over a number of days. It is clear from Egeria that in fourth-century Jerusalem separate liturgical commemorations had developed for Jesus' 'triumphal entry' into the city, his last days of teaching, confrontation with the authorities, last supper in the context of Passover, arrest and trial, crucifixion, burial and resurrection. For example, when Egeria recounts the Good Friday commemorations, she suggests that:

> The bishop's chair is placed on Golgotha Behind the Cross (the cross there now), and he takes his seat. A table is placed before him with a cloth on it, the deacons stand round, and there is brought to him a gold and silver box containing the holy Wood of the Cross. It is opened, and the Wood of the Cross and the Title are taken out and placed on the table. As long as the holy Wood is on the table, the bishop sits with his hands resting on either end of it and holds it down, and the deacons round him keep watch over it. They guard it like this because what happens now is that all the people,

catechumens as well as faithful, come up one by one to the table. They stoop down over it, kiss the Wood, and move on. But on one occasion (I don't know when) one of them bit off a piece of the holy Wood and stole it away, and for this reason the deacons stand round and keep watch in case anyone dares to do the same again. They stoop down, touch the holy Wood first with their forehead and then with their eyes, and then kiss it, but no one puts out his hands to touch it.[8]

After this service, another follows: a three-hour word service, of readings, in which biblical passages are set alongside one another to illumine promise and fulfilment in Christ. At 3 o'clock, John's Gospel account of Jesus giving up the ghost concludes the sequence of readings, and is followed by simple prayer and dismissal. In the evening, another service is conducted at what was believed to be the site of Jesus' tomb, at which Matthew 27.57–61 is read.

Egeria's records of the various services held throughout the 'Great Week' have provided blueprints for subsequent liturgical celebration of these days and are still key to the shape and content of worship in Holy Week in a number of Christian traditions.

A distinctive aspect of Good Friday liturgy, to which Egeria gives the first witness, are the 'reproaches' as a particular way of appropriating the meaning of the passion of Jesus. Egeria tells of prayers taking place which imagine the crucified saviour pleading with his people from the cross, beginning with the recitation of Lamentations 1.17, transferred to Jesus' mouth. Long a part of Catholic devotion on the Friday of Holy Week, the reproaches have recently enjoyed a greater role in some Protestant traditions, and here is a version from the United Methodist Church of the USA:

Is it nothing to you, all you who pass by?
Look and see if there is any sorrow like my sorrow
Which was brought upon me,
Which the Lord inflicted on the day of his fierce anger.
O my people, o my church,
What have I done to you,
Or in what have I offended you?
Testify against me.

I led you forth from the land of Egypt
And delivered you by the waters of baptism,
But you have prepared a cross for your savior.
I led you through the desert forty years,
And fed you with manna:
I brought you through tribulation and penitence,
And gave you my body, the bread of heaven,
But you have prepared a cross for your savior.
What more could I have done for you
That I have not done?
I planted you, my chosen and fairest vineyard,
I made you the branches of my vine;
But when I was thirsty, you gave me vinegar to drink
And pierced with a spear the side of your savior.
I went before you in a pillar of cloud,
And you have led me to the judgment hall of Pilate.
I scourged your enemies and brought you to a land of freedom,
But you have scourged, mocked, and beaten me.
I gave you the water of salvation from the rock,
But you have given me gall and left me to thirst.
I gave you a royal scepter,
And bestowed the keys to the kingdom,
But you have given me a crown of thorns.
I raised you on high with great power,
But you have hanged me on a cross.
My peace I gave, which the world cannot give,
And washed your feet as a sign of my love,
But you draw the sword to strike in my name
And seek high places in my kingdom.
I offered you my body and blood,
But you scatter and deny and abandon me.
I sent the Spirit of truth to guide you,
And you close your hearts to the Counselor.
I pray that all may be one in the Father and me,
But you continue to quarrel and divide.

I call you to go and bring forth fruit,
But you cast lots for my clothing.
I grafted you into the tree of my chosen Israel,
And you turned on them with persecution and mass murder.
I made you joint heirs with them of my covenants,
But you made them scapegoats for your own guilt.
I came to you as the least of your brothers and sisters;
I was hungry and you gave me no food,
I was thirsty and you gave me no drink,
I was a stranger and you did not welcome me,
Naked and you did not clothe me,
Sick and in prison and you did not visit me.[9]

The reproaches can be regarded as 'an inversion of the holy history we recite and recall in the Great Thanksgiving at the Lord's table',[10] although they tend to generate very different kinds of reaction. On the one hand, Gail Ramshaw writes of her appreciation of the ways in which the reproaches resist contemporary individualism – as she asks, 'My story, my story – aren't we all getting sick of my story?' In contrast to contemporary endemic emphasis on the individual, the reproaches, she asserts, invite participants in liturgy into imaginative identification with Israel, with saints and sinners down the ages; to be 'not merely me, but mythically more':

Good Friday can be for Christians another exercise of the I. I am unworthy. I will die. I had better meditate on Jesus, another loner. I am walled up in my grief over the past year's deaths. I am alone on my knees. And into my solitary confinement flows the waters of the Red Sea. We are swept into that story of other people's death and life, their suffering and God's mercy to them. Ha, says the Reproaches! Today is not only about you and the dying Jesus. Today is about all the world's people: listen to Moses cry, hear Miriam sing . . .[11]

In this, the reproaches do much as the intercessions are intended to do – remember the whole world, stretching concern well beyond the self. And the reproaches assert that this day makes all the difference to the hopes and fears of the whole human family. On the other hand, the reproaches remain subject to various critiques, perhaps most powerfully that of the ex-Dominican Jacques Pohier. He writes of growing into his conviction that 'the reproaches put in the mouth of God were not at all like what we had heard half an hour earlier [in the Scripture readings of the Good Friday liturgy] in those few words which the evangelist had put on the lips of Jesus, not to mention the silence which he had made him observe'.[12] The contrast between the silence of the Gospels – notably the silence of Jesus in the Gospels' stories of the cross – is, for Pohier, a strong corrective to the reproaches' images of what Pohier calls the 'complaining' of Jesus:

> Each reading of the passion has confirmed this impression for me: Jesus had been silent; he had not complained by constantly saying 'O my people, what have I done for you?'; he had not made a catalogue of all his good deeds in order to overwhelm us with shame by cataloguing our misdeeds. He did not humiliate us; he was himself humiliated, and in a far different way from that which we associate with him. Certainly, he had complained, but as a man who was suffering, not as a man giving a lesson of listing what his debtors owe him . . .[13]

For Pohier, the reproaches are emphatically 'out of place given all we know of God as [they are] out of place given the little we know about genuine forgiveness'![14] Both Ramshaw and Pohier's perspectives offer much to think about in considering how the reproaches might or might not find a place in opening up the meaning of Good Friday; they are reminders not least of the ways in which liturgies inform and shape theology, mission and the message Christians have to share; and they suggest either how welcome or how complex appropriating Egeria's legacy may be.

In their contemporary celebration, Lent and Easter stand dynamically alongside each other as contrasting seasons. Don Saliers calls the movement through them one 'from ashes to fire': from the ashen-faced penitential emphasis of Ash Wednesday through to the 'burning hearts' of the disciples on the way to Emmaus in one of the mysterious first accounts of Jesus' resurrection, through to the wild 'tongues of flame' associated with the Spirit's empowerment of the disciples' witness on the day of Pentecost. The motif 'from ashes to fire' is helpful for gesturing the kind of contrasts yielded by these seasons. But considered individually, the seasons also contain fascinating contrasts, as in Alexander Schmemann's exposition of Lent as a time of 'bright sadness':

> ... an 'atmosphere', a 'climate' into which one enters, first of all a state of mind, soul and spirit which for seven weeks permeates our entire life.... The purpose of Lent is not to force on us a few formal obligations, but to 'soften' our heart so that it may open itself to the realities of the spirit, to experience the hidden 'hunger and thirst' for communion with God.
>
> This Lenten 'atmosphere', this unique 'state of mind', is brought about mainly by means of worship, by the various changes introduced during the season into the liturgical life. Considered separately, these changes may appear as incomprehensible 'rubrics', as formal prescriptions to be formally adhered to; but understood as a whole, they reveal and communicate the spirit of Lent, they make us see, feel, and experience bright sadness which is the true message and gift of Lent ...
>
> The general impression . . . is that of 'bright sadness'. Even [someone] who enters a church for the first time during a lenten service would understand almost immediately, I am sure, what is meant by this somewhat contradictory expression. On the one hand, a certain quiet sadness permeates the services: vestments are dark, the services are longer than usual and more monotonous, there is almost no movement . . . But then we begin to realize that this very length and monotony are needed if we are to experience the secret and at first unnoticeable 'action' of the service in us. Little by little we begin to understand, or rather to feel, that this sadness is indeed bright, that a mysterious transformation is about to take place in us ...
>
> 'Sad brightness': the sadness of my exile, of the waste I have made of my life; the brightness of God's presence and forgiveness, the joy of the recovered desire for God, the peace of the restored home. Such is the climate of Lenten worship . . .[15]

Considering the lectionary for the two contrasting seasons is a profound way to gain insight into the dynamics of the seasons. They lead scripture readers on a journey through a number of moods and contrasts – into the realization of the depths of sin and then into discovery and delight in Christ's presence; Lent exploring the shadows of the human condition, Easter glorying in the attractiveness of Christ. In the Lenten readings for year A, for instance, after introducing the mercy of Jesus shown to the adulterous woman (John 8.1–11), there is then some strong dealing with our need of mercy. The readings face us with the bleakness of wrestling with temptation (Matt. 4.1–11), the need to be born again (John 3.1–17), the search to quench our thirst (John 4.5–42), pharisaical blindness (John 9.1–41), deadness and grief (John 11.10–45). In Easter year A, Christ invites encounter: as the familiar stranger in the garden (John 20.1–18), the living one marked by nails (John 20.19–31), the encouraging teacher on the journey, the surprising host (Luke 24.13–35), the strong good shepherd (John 10.1–10), the way, the truth and the life in the spacious presence of God (John 14.1–14), the consoler and sender of the coming 'other comforter', the Spirit (John 14.15–21). Both seasons and their respective patterns of readings suggest a pathway to conversion.

This conversion emphasis is also central to how recent renewal of the seasons of Lent and Easter has been linked with revision of initiation rites – especially those relating to baptism – which have recovered the early church's sense of Lent as the time for catechesis. The classic example of recovery of these ancient patterns of teaching is the remarkable Roman Catholic *Rite of Christian Initiation of Adults*, which was developed after the reforms of the Second Vatican Council, drawing mostly on fourth-century models of evangelism. Like the lectionary readings of Lent and Easter, it provides a way to be transformed, ritualizing in highly experiential events various stages of response to the gospel. Many Protestant traditions have adopted some of its emphases – some staging ritualized processes of catechesis, as in the United States Anglican prayerbooks – while almost universally, the motif of 'journey' has been embraced as key to understanding initiation, with consideration now given to the whole process of contact, invitation, teaching, response and after-care around baptism.[16]

The Sense of the Christmas Cycle

The next major part of the Christian year to develop was that around Christmas, the celebration of Jesus' birth. The origins of Christmas day itself are interesting, though vague. Still, they are not without challenge for the church in the context of its contemporary mission.

It seems that 25 December has been designated Christmas day, at least in the West (in the East, the day has been celebrated on 6 or January), since AD 336. There are two main theories about the identification of 25 December as Christmas day, and the two theories may overlap. Put simply, one centres around the date of the winter solstice. Since AD 274, 25 December had been a festival of the 'unconquered sun'. The Christian church may have adopted this day as a piece of combative evangelism, and used it to proclaim Jesus as the 'sun of righteousness' (Mal. 4.2) who outshines other suns! That day by day – at least in the northern hemisphere – the light increases in the days following Christmas, may have underscored the idea of Jesus as the light. Note that the festival became embedded in Christian practice at around the time of the controversies behind the Nicene Creed – its various references to 'light' suggest the practical alliances of theology and devotional practice. (And reflecting similar dynamics to the date of Christmas, the designation of 1 January as a day of Mary, as still in the Roman Catholic tradition, may well also have been a way of contesting the pagan new year.)

Put simply, the other theory leans more into Christianity's Jewish background, and picks up the Jewish notion of significant persons being born and dying on the same date of the year. Since the time of Hippolytus, Good Friday had at least in some places been identified as 25 March, thought to correspond to Nissan 14, and so, it was thought, this day must also be the date of Jesus' origins. Note that the date of his birth is deduced from the supposed date of his conception, which was the Christian twist to this Jewish idea. (25 March remains a day of celebration of Mary in many Christian traditions – *Common Worship* designates it as 'The Annunciation of Our Lord to the Blessed Virgin Mary'.)

The Christmas season develops themes that are concentrated in Christmas day itself. The season of Christmas runs from Christmas eve to Epiphany,

6 January (think of the '12 days of Christmas'), and Christmastide itself belongs to a larger context – Advent to Candlemas/Presentation of Christ in the Temple (2 February). The stories of Jesus' birth have harsh aspects like the travail of journeying and expressions of exclusion, and the season includes and amplifies these. Something of the stretch of themes all located in the season can be seen by considering the calendar of saints for the days immediately following Christmas day. They commemorate Stephen (26 December), John (27 December) and the Holy Innocents (28 December). In the Middle Ages, these feasts were designated 'Companions of Christ', seen to mark three ways of accompanying Christ in martyrdom. Together, they point to an 'underside' in the Christmas season – bleak, harsh realities that sometimes do not find acknowledgement in sentimental celebrations of Christmas in our contemporary culture. The presence of such themes in the season of Christmas raises contemporary questions about how churches resist or collude with sentimental celebrations of Christmas, making it more palatable or insisting on its 'edge'.

Within the wider context of the Christmas season, 6 January is another major focus. (It is still marked as Christmas day in the Eastern Christian traditions.) From early days, in the West this day was associated with the baptism of Christ, relating Jesus' birth to the symbolism of new birth granted to believers in Jesus. This date was fixed perhaps in part in another piece of combative evangelism, contesting the pagan commemoration on 6 January of the birth of Aion, god of time and eternity, in whose memory water was drawn from the Nile. So in focusing on this day, the church may have been making a bold statement about time and eternity being the gift and subject of Jesus.

Another strand within the season is the sequence from 17 December through to 6 January, which maps onto the pagan celebration known as saturnalia. The early contest with saturnalia, which was marked by excess and debauchery, led to the church to require from Christian people an increased asceticism of devotion and practice through these days. In this, and perhaps in the ways that saints' days came to be set alongside the celebration of the nativity, there are important precedents for resisting what Haddon Willmer calls the 'commercialism, nostalgia and sentimentality about God and humanity lead us annual bouts of misrepresenting Christian faith with the false hope that Christianity can be built on keeping children happy'.[17] The history of Christmas offers strong incentives to critical engagement with dominant culture.

Liturgy and the Life-Cycle

Liturgy has sometimes been called 'the most important form of pastoral care'. This claim relates in part to the various resources of the tradition of Christian worship for the cycles and crises of the human lifetime, particularly the seven sacraments of Catholic tradition: baptism, confirmation, eucharist, reconciliation (or penance), marriage, orders, and the sacrament of the sick. One way of understanding the seven sacraments is as corresponding to many of the joys and sorrows of human being – as enabling celebration of the very grace of being (baptism), the adult choice of a paschal identity (confirmation), Christ-centred self-giving (communion), faithful life-partnership (marriage), the restoration of brokenness (reconciliation/penance), the embrace of frailty (sacrament of the sick), and wholehearted attentiveness to the other (orders).

The various doctrinal streams of Christianity have embraced these rites as sacraments in different measure. For example, some traditions – such as the Anglican tradition – have affirmed baptism and eucharist as 'gospel sacraments', while regarding the other five as 'common sacraments' (Article 25) of lesser status. Some Protestant traditions have at times also found at least as weighty gospel mandate for other sacraments of the Catholic tradition as they have done for baptism and communion, and Luther's own early affirmation of penance is a case in point. However, most Protestant traditions tend to acknowledge only two sacraments – baptism and eucharist – as being instituted by Jesus in the Gospels. For centuries, Matthew's memory of Jesus' command to 'go and make disciples of all nations, baptizing them in the name of the Father and of the Son and of the Holy Spirit' (Matt. 28.19) and Luke and Paul's account of Jesus' words over bread and wine at the last supper, to 'do this' (Luke 22.19; 1 Cor. 11.24–25), were taken as the Lord's own mandate to the church. In more recent times, some reserve has emerged about ascribing these mandates to Jesus himself, not least because the trinitarian formula from Matthew appears to be a later insertion which reflects an era of more fixed doctrinal understanding about the relations of the divine persons than is present anywhere else in the records of Jesus' own speech and teaching. Hence, traditional claims to dominical institution are less certain than in previous centuries.

In contemporary Roman Catholic sacramental theology, the 'institution' of sacraments tends to be rooted in the notion of Christ himself as the 'primary sacrament' who makes divine reality visible as revealer of the meaning of particular sacraments as: the baptized one (baptism), confirmed one (confirmation), really present one (eucharist), reconciler (penance), priest (orders), lover (marriage) and healer (anointing); and minister of each. As Bernard Cooke writes:

> Jesus did not 'institute the sacraments' by initiating certain religious rituals himself. Instead, he gave to the entirety of human existence a new significance, because he lived and died and rose to life under the constant impact of God's intimate presence. God, Jesus' Abba, dwelt with him in unparalleled immediacy, so early Christianity saw Jesus as 'the new temple'. Jesus was a living embodiment of this saving divine presence, for he was God's own Word, the sacrament of God's saving power in human history.
>
> Though the whole of Jesus' life was sacramental, special significance attached to his death and resurrection. In experiencing death as the free acceptance of ultimate risk, as complete fidelity to truth and love, as supreme witness to his Abba, and as passage into new life, Jesus gave human existence its full and final significance. This is the Christ-meaning expressed in the Christian sacraments as they trans-signify human life. Jesus instituted these sacraments by being – in life, death, and resurrection – the primordial sacrament of his Father's saving presence.[18]

These various perspectives point to the fact that notions of the sacramental have always had a measure of flexibility, indeed the seven of Catholic tradition were only fixed in the eleventh century, whereas for many centuries a great many actions, rites and exchanges were regarded as sacramental: '"sacrament" could cover the Lord's prayer, the creed, the liturgy, the sign of the cross, the font of baptism, the water used, ashes, oil, blessing, foot-washing, the reading and exposition of scripture and prayers',[19] while others with strong claim to 'dominical institution' in the sense of being recorded in the Gospels – such as footwashing – were never later incorporated into the Catholic sacramental structure of the second millennium.

While Protestant traditions may not recognize the sacramental status of rites other than baptism and eucharist, corresponding neither to the Catholic seven nor the early expansiveness of the idea, they do however all tend to focus the care of persons around the moments touched by the seven sacraments. The Protestant traditions have continued to provide rites, and locate pastoral attention, around the experiences of the life-cycle to which the Catholic seven correspond. For example, as noted, penance was retained in very early Lutheranism, and it survives in certain liturgical forms in both Lutheran and Anglican practice (less so in English Anglicanism than in other provinces, interestingly). Cranmer's problems with the rite were largely about its unfortunate capacity to bulwark understandings of a sacerdotal priesthood in which he could not believe, hence his shifting confession into the arena of public worship: very strong echoes of the Book of Common Prayer's confession are still found in one of the *Common Worship* confessions: 'we acknowledge and bewail our manifold sins and wickedness . . . the rememberence of them is grievous unto us; the burden of them intolerable'.[20] And Thomas Oden argues that the tradition of pastoral visiting grew up as a characteristically Protestant response to the demise of private sacramental confession, effectively its replacement as a means of offering care around the personal issues of guilt and forgiveness.[21] In later Protestant history, the rise of pastoral counselling became perhaps the key means by which Protestant ministers came to engage these issues, effectively establishing a kind of rival confessional while ditching the language of sacramentality. Indeed, it was the eventual, alleged, 'therapeutic captivity' of Protestant pastoral care that led Oden to rediscover and re-evaluate – positively – the 'classical tradition' of penance and its reconfiguration in early Protestantism as a way of contesting the growing emphasis on pale imitations of professional therapy.

If the seven sacraments are important and durable foci for consideration of pastoral care, they are also important in terms of evangelism. James White rightly suggests that 'for the marginal Christian – and there are millions of alumni and alumnae of the churches – weddings and funerals may be the only link to the worshiping community. In terms of evangelization the rites of passage may be even more important than the Eucharist.'[22]

Baptism

Also key to mission is engagement in baptism. Unlike the 'common sacraments', baptism is practised across the Christian traditions, with the exception of only the Salvation Army and the Quakers. It is, of course, rooted in the experience of Jesus, who was himself baptized at the beginning of his public ministry. The Gospels relate some confusion about whether or not Jesus himself actually then baptized others – John 4.2 seeming to stamp on the rumour of John 3.22. However, an interesting fragment of an apocryphal gospel has recently been recovered which offers a hint of Jesus as baptizer, although it is as yet uncertain what kind of historical authenticity can be ascribed to it. The Secret Gospel of Mark claims to be catechetical material given to new converts in addition to the public version of the Gospel of Mark, and it includes following Mark 10.34:

> And they came to Bethany. And a certain women whose brother had died was there. And, coming, she prostrated herself before Jesus and says to him, 'Son of David, have mercy on me.' But the disciples rebuked her. And Jesus, being angered, went off with her into the garden where to the tomb was, and straightaway a great cry was heard from the tomb. And going near Jesus rolled away the stone from the door of the tomb. And straightaway, going in where the youth was, he stretched forth his hand and raised him, seizing his hand. But the youth, looking upon him, loved him and began to beseech him that he might be with him. And going out of the tomb they came out of the house of the youth, for he was rich. And after six days Jesus told him what to do and in the evening the youth comes to him, wearing a linen cloth over his naked body. And he remained with him that night, for Jesus taught him the mystery of the kingdom of God. And thence, arising, he returned to the other side of the Jordan . . .[23]

Early church records of baptisms reflect the kind of ambiguities that surround

Jesus' own baptismal practice, or not, and it is clear at least that there was considerable variety in the way that initiation was approached. The New Testament reflects a chaotic approach in the apostolic and early period about the order in which new believers submitted to baptism in water, received the laying on of hands, and anointing by the Holy Spirit; about the age of baptismal candidates in the apostolic period – including the crucial question of whether or not this embraced children; and about the images used to unfold the meaning of baptism. The important World Council of Churches document on *Baptism, Eucharist and Ministry* collates some of the many and varied pieces of scriptural witness as to the meaning of baptism as follows:

> Baptism is participation in Christ's death and resurrection (Rom. 6.3–5; Col. 2.12); a washing away of sin (1 Cor. 6.11); a new birth (John 3.5); an enlightenment by Christ (Eph. 5.14); a reclothing in Christ (Gal. 3.27); a renewal by the Spirit (Titus 3.5); an experience of salvation from the flood (1 Pet. 3.20–21); an exodus from bondage (1 Cor. 10.1–2) and a liberation into a new humanity in which barriers of division whether of sex or race or social status are transcended (Gal. 3.27–28; 1 Cor. 12.13).

It concludes, however, that 'the images are many but the reality is one',[24] and the diversity of subsequent approaches to baptism in the history of the church can in many ways be seen as a reflection of the multiplicity of perspectives to be found in the Bible:

> Dear Miss Manners,
> What is the proper age for baptism?
>
> Gentle Reader:
> It varies, depending on a variety of factors. For example, have you just been born or were you born again?[25]

One of the main points of controversy in the history of baptismal practice has been over the appropriate age for baptism. New Testament references to 'household' baptisms suggest that children were included, as all associated with the patriarchal head-of-household are likely to have been. Certainly, by the third century, the baptism of children was standard practice, although this followed an earlier trend towards 'death-bed' baptism, deferred until just before death due to fears that post-baptismal sin could not be forgiven.

While infant baptism was undoubtedly the majority practice for several subsequent centuries, considerable controversy opened up at the Reformation as some radical reformers excluded children from baptism, concerned that it should be practised as a response to the personal appropriation of faith. The legacy of their arguments are still to be found in Baptist, Christian Brethren, and Pentecostal traditions. For example, it is enshrined in the 'declaration of principle' made by public ministers in the Baptist tradition: 'That Christian baptism is the immersion in water into the name of the Father, the Son and the Holy Ghost, of those who have professed repentance towards God and faith in our Lord Jesus Christ who "died for our sins according to the Scriptures; was buried, and rose again the third day".'[26] The majority of reformers continued the practice of infant baptism, however, as in the words of the Articles of Religion of the emerging Church of England, which affirm infant baptism as 'most agreeable with the institution of Christ' (Article 27). Most Christian traditions now baptize both adults and children, about which the World Council of Churches' *Baptism, Eucharist and Ministry* identifies some of the characteristics which are common to both: they both 'take place in the community of faith', both are 'rooted in and declare . . . Christ's faithfulness unto death', and, crucially, 'in both cases the baptized person will have to grow in understanding of faith'.[27] At least some of the problems that believer-baptizing communities continue to have with infant baptism are eased by recognition that 'both forms of baptism require a similar and responsible attitude towards Christian nurture'.[28]

In the contemporary cultural climate, baptism of either infants or adults is increasingly perceived as an opportunity for mission. For example, with the baptism of both adults and children in mind, this is affirmed in the first statement of the worldwide Anglican statement on baptism, *Walk in Newness of Life*: 'The renewal of baptismal practice is an integral part of mission and evangelism. Liturgical texts must point beyond the life of the church to God's mission in the world.'[29] And, furthermore, it is increasingly assumed that the regular worshipping congregation will be present at every baptism to surround and support the newly baptized, either adult or infant. In this regard, the *Common Worship* order of baptism for the Church of England includes a new feature in the following, addressed to the 'whole congregation':

> Faith is the gift of God to his people.
> In baptism the Lord is adding to our number
> those whom he is calling.
>   People of God, will you welcome these children/candidates
> and uphold them in their new life in Christ?

To which all respond: 'With the help of God we will'.[30] On the need for the assembly's presence, Elaine Ramshaw writes:

> On this point there has been widespread ecumenical agreement: it is important to restore baptism to the Sunday assembly in order to make it clear that baptism is not just an infant blessing, a life-cycle rite affecting the baby and his or her immediate family, but an incorporation into the body of Christ. The wider gathered community represents more adequately the entire body of Christ, the whole communion of saints, into which the child is being baptized. On the one hand, it is important for the baby's family and godparents to realize this larger community claims their child – both so that they may take seriously the communal nature of living the faith and so that they may experience the community's support in the task of rearing the child in the faith. On the other hand, it is necessary for the congregation to realize how it is implicated in the child's baptism, for a rite of passage into a community is a rite of passage for the whole community.[31]

Indeed, Ramshaw suggests that this translates as a challenge to congregations that might be expressed as: 'this is our new sister; you'd better get to know her, because you're responsible for her now'![32]

An important feature of new rites of baptism is the inclusion of personal statements to those being baptized. Here is an example from the Church of Scotland's *Book of Common Order* which has provided a model for similar prayers across different traditions in Britain:

> N . . . for you Jesus Christ came into the world:
> for you he lived and showed God's love;

for you he suffered the darkness of Calvary
and cried at the last 'It is accomplished';
for you he triumphed over the death and rose in newness of life;
for you he ascended to reign at God's right hand.
All this he did for you, N,
though you did not know it yet.
and so the word of Scripture is fulfilled,
'We love because God first loved us'.
[Parents and godparents], tell her of her baptism
and unfold to her the treasure she has been given today.[33]

This prayer is adjusted in a Methodist prayer to speak more clearly to both adults and children. A similar prayer in the English Anglican *Common Worship* also employs the imagery of 'journey' that is now central to the whole baptismal rite, and indeed the whole of its 'pastoral services'.[34] As already mentioned, the emphasis on journey and growth over time draws deeply on the example of the Roman Catholic *Rite of Christian Initiation of Adults*.

One very important feature of recent liturgical renewal has been the sense of the importance of recovering a focus on baptism and allowing for 'baptismal renewal'. Undoubtedly, one of the unforeseen and unintended results of renewal of attention to the eucharist in many Christian traditions has been the decline in other sources and modes of worship. We have noted Gordon Wakefield's caution to 'beware of impoverishment' that may ensue when the eucharist becomes central, however desirable that in itself may be. That celebration of the eucharist involves attention to both word and table has not always been appreciated, and the recovery of baptism is especially important given that it can also claim a vital place in the celebration of a sacramental spirituality. Numerous resources are now being developed to better enable congregations to celebrate the renewal of baptism, though this is best seen as a means of recovering a focus that has been lost rather than never previously present. For example, Philip Pfatteicher writes:

No one has written more powerfully and eloquently of the eternal significance of baptism than Martin Luther. The principal glory of

Lutheran theology is its profound understanding of the nature, power and duration of Holy Baptism. Baptism consists of preparation, presentation, thanksgiving, renunciation of evil and profession of faith in the triune God, baptism in water, laying on of hands and signation with the cross, welcome into the congregation and church, instruction in the mysteries of the faith, living, confessing and receiving forgiveness, dying, sharing in the resurrection. For, as Luther wrote in his gleaming essay *The Holy and Blessed Sacrament of Baptism* (1519), baptism is not fulfilled completely in this life. The physical baptism is quickly over, but the spiritual baptism, the drowning of sin, which it signifies, lasts as long as we live and is completed only in death. Then it is that a person is completely sunk in baptism and that which baptism signifies, the death of the old nature, comes to pass. 'Those who are baptized are condemned to die, and therefore this whole life is nothing else than a spiritual baptism which does not cease till death' (*Luther's Works* 35.30) ... The drowning, the dying of baptism lasts as long as we live. So too the rising from the water, the spiritual birth, continues until death ...[35]

Related perspectives can be found in Calvin: 'All pious folk throughout life, whenever they are troubled by a consciousness of their faults, may venture to remind themselves of their baptism, that from it they be confirmed in assurance of that sole and perpetual cleansing which we have in Christ's blood'.[36] We have seen a Reformed attempt to enable congregations to recover refreshment of baptism in the Uniting Church in Australia's liturgy cited in Chapter 2; equally creative things exist within, for example, the United Church of Canada; and within British Methodism, where every celebration of baptism now involves the praying of the following congregational prayer:

Generous God,
touch us again with the fire of your Spirit
and renew in us all the grace of our Baptism,
that we might profess the one true faith
and live in love and unity
with all who are baptized into Christ. Amen.[37]

Within the Church of England, a thanksgiving for baptism is included in

Common Worship for use at services of the word, and this as well as seasonal rites (e.g. for the celebration of the baptism of Christ) promote the aspersion of the assembly: 'The water may be sprinkled over the people or they may be invited to use it to sign themselves with the cross'.[38] Creative reflections on the structure of the eucharistic liturgy commend the use of aspersion in the invitation to repentance at holy communion, which need not depend on altering any liturgical text. Richard Giles suggests that the Sunday assembly's invitation to repentance and absolution might be held at the font,[39] which is an interesting variation on one of the options for the gathering rite of the Roman Catholic mass, in which the gathering may emphasize either peni-tence or baptismal remembrance. Giles argues that the two are related: in the prayers of penitence, 'the people may come to the font one by one, to dip their finger in the water and to make the sign of the cross on themselves, or better still, make the sign on the cross on each other, as an interactive symbol of God's choosing and God's forgiveness'.[40] And whatever form the penitential rite may take, above all Giles commends regular 'gathering at the well':

> In many church buildings, to gather around the existing font is almost a practical impossibility, but do it nevertheless. Do it when only a few can get within touching distance, do it with people standing on pews or sitting on window sills. Do it until the cry goes up, 'How long, O Lord, how long ... before we can build a proper font?' ... Even the meanest, silliest, little bird bath, or the ugliest brute of a monster, can be a (temporary) reprieve if you take off (and lose) its lid, and fill it with water until it overflows ...[41]

Giles' advice points to a crucial dimension of contemporary attempts to enliven baptism among congregations: the growing emphasis on enlarging both the vessels and gestures of baptism. 'A proper font', these days, might well consist of a pool large enough in which to submerge an adult, and employ the sound of running water, so that an audible echo of baptism is part of the liturgical environment as well as a stronger visible focus.[42] Such fonts, unlike the kind of baptisteries used in many Baptist churches, are not hidden away under floorboards when not in use, but are a focus of attention week by week. Their 'use' is not only in allowing for baptism itself, but in enabling the congregation week by week to embrace a baptismal spirituality.

The rise of new forms of baptismal renewal has in turn been part of reconsidering confirmation. It is fair to say that across a number of traditions, confirmation is currently regarded as 'a rite without a theology' – sometimes, with the widespread conviction that baptism admits to the Lord's table, now needing to be radically revised. Increasingly, confirmation is currently being reconfigured as an adult affirmation of commissioning to ministry with a strong emphasis on personal testimony to divine grace and intent to embody a life of witness. To that end, some provinces of the Anglican Communion now tie the title 'confirmation' to 'commissioning', as in 'Confirmation and Commissioning' in the Anglican Church of Kenya service. In Kenya, the promises made by candidates are as follows:

> We, about to be commissioned
> for the mission of Christ and his Church,
> pledge to keep and walk in God's commandments
> all the days of our lives,
> and to read the Bible and pray regularly.
> We pledge to proclaim Christ,
> in season and out of season,
> to obey him and to live in the fellowship
> of all true believers throughout the world.
> We pledge to be active in church,
> to give to the work of the church,
> to help the needy, support the poor,
> and to be good stewards of all that the Lord has given to us.
> We pledge to uphold truth and justice,
> and to seek reconciliation among all people;
> the Lord being our helper.[43]

This is a strong expression of a shift that can be found elsewhere, such as in the Church of England's *Common Worship* forms, in which the affirmations made by candidates for confirmation may also be recalled in services of the word which focus particularly on 'thanksgiving for the mission of the church',[44] as well as being able to be used on other occasions as an affirmation of commitment in addition to a creed or authorized affirmation of faith:[45]

Will you continue in the apostles' teaching and fellowship,
in the breaking of bread and in the prayers?
With the help of God, I will.
Will you persevere in resisting evil, and
whenever you fall into sin, repent and return to the Lord?
With the help of God, I will.
Will you proclaim by word and example
the good news of God in Christ?
With the help of God, I will.
Will you seek and serve Christ in all people,
loving your neighbour as yourself?
With the help of God, I will.
Will you acknowledge Christ's authority over human society,
by prayer for the world and its leaders,
by defending the weak, and by seeking peace and justice?
With the help of God, I will.

The strong ethical dimension of such questions is a recovery of the moral seriousness with which initiation was regarded in the early centuries:

> In the first centuries of Christianity, seekers were required not just to profess their belief in Jesus as the Christ, but to make choices about their daily lives. The profession of Christian faith they would eventually be invited to make was not a matter merely of repeating doctrinal formulas, but was something to be tested in the crucible of daily life itself. Conversion of life was seen in how one related to others, in how one earned a living, in how one could be trusted.[46]

Hymnody for the celebration of baptism is also developing, a good example of which is Susan Palo Cherwien's 'O Blessed Spring', which sings of return to the waters of baptism at different stages of life – the 'summer heat of youth', the 'cooling autumn' of age, the winter of death, and resurrection as 'springtime', into which baptism initiated in the first place.[47]

Michael Perham writes that

> If the twentieth century was the century of the recovery of the meaning of the eucharist for the Church, bringing it back into the centre of Christian

life and worship in a way that had not been the case at least in the Reformed Churches, so that people began to understand that their formation was all bound up with being eucharistic people, there is a case to be made that the twenty-first century may witness a parallel recovery of the meaning of baptism for the Church.[48]

If baptism is indeed integral to the church's mission, very much may depend on whether or not Perham turns out to be right.

Gordon Lathrop sets an expansive agenda for what renewal of baptism might involve:

From the beginning, baptism has held more than one thing together in a lively tension. It takes place once, yet it is for all of our life. It is for living, yet it is also for dying. It happens to individuals; indeed, it graciously celebrates individual persons. Yet it constitutes a community, is an event for the community. It is an utter gift of grace, a thing that can never be earned or learned. Yet it calls for conversion, for discipleship, for teaching the faith, for lifelong learning. It happens in a single, great washing. Yet it rightly unfolds in a ritual process. It has occurred through twenty centuries in many different places, with all the waters of the world: in Mediterranean pools, in the African surf, and even with North American hospital eye-droppers. Yet there is only 'one baptism' (Ephesians 4.5).

In its utter grace, baptism is for infants but also for adults. In its realism about death and its good news about hope in Christ, baptism is for adults but also for infants. Indeed, we baptize infants as if they were adults, addressing them and according them great dignity, and adults as if they were infants, washing them and drying them off and holding them with tender care.

These paradoxes or ambiguities of baptism exist, of course, because baptism is anchored in Jesus Christ. We believe that his death is life. His once-for-all coming gives a universal meaning to the world and is already God's intended end for the world. In him, the wiping away of all tears and the doing of all justice –the promises of God's day – have already begun, yet they are still coming. In him, all the diverse created things hold together and all persons – infants and adults, men and women, rich and poor, those from both east and west – are endowed with the Spirit and stand before

God in great dignity. Jesus Christ and the faith that is through him, is utter gift, yet that gift takes a lifetime to learn. His word addresses each one; his word forms his body, the church.

Thus the bath that is enacted in his name is as he is, holding opposites together in mercy and grace . . . Renewal in the present time will be the stronger as we restore the rich tensions of baptism. Can we make the once-for-all washing a stronger, more consequential event, and, at the same time, rediscover baptism's meaning for daily living? Can we accentuate grace and still claim the necessary enacting of a process in this rite of passage – a process with its welcoming and blessing and forming of the candidates? Can we baptize adults with new strength and still baptize infants with joy? Can we newly emphasise the roles of sponsors and godparents and congregation and still bless individual responsibility? Can we accentuate baptism as entrance into Christ and his community while offering an overwhelming welcome to all outsiders, ourselves included? Can baptism form this congregation and still be our link with all the churches of Christ? . . .[49]

Conclusion

In this chapter we have touched upon some aspects of the manifold relationships between liturgy and time. There are many reasons for considering these relationships, although one of the most important must be that each one is significant for the mission of the church. Sunday orientates worshippers to witness to resurrection. The seasons of the Christian year, most notably Christmas, developed in relation to witness to the wider societies in which the early church was set. The church's rites at nodal points in the human life-cycle provide opportunity not only for pastoral care but demand attention as occasions for evangelism in so far as they are sometimes the main opportunities for the church to offer hospitality to those who are not closely involved in Sunday worship. Most of the chapter has been concerned with baptism, however, because the recovery of its centrality and missionary significance in the life of the church is perhaps, above all, a challenge the churches must embrace for their future flourishing.

Further Reading

Francis-Louis Chavet, *The Sacraments: The Word of God at the Mercy of the Body* (Collegeville, MN: Liturgical Press, 2003).

James Farwell, *This Is the Night: Suffering, Salvation and the Liturgies of Holy Week* (New York: Continuum, 2005).

Maxwell E. Johnson (ed.), *Between Memory and Hope: Readings on the Liturgical Year* (Collegeville, MN: Liturgical Press, 2000).

Maxwell E. Johnson (ed.), *Documents of the Baptismal Liturgy* (London: SPCK, 2003).

Maxwell E. Johnson, *Rites of Christian Initiation* (Collegeville, MN: Liturgical Press, 1999).

John Macquarrie, *A Guide to the Sacraments* (London: SCM Press, 1997).

German Martinez, *Signs of Freedom: Theology of the Christian Sacraments* (New York: Paulist Press, 2000).

Geoffrey Rowell and Christine Hall (eds), *The Gestures of God: Explorations in Sacramentality* (London: Continuum, 2004).

Thomas J. Talley, *The Origins of the Liturgical Year* (Collegeville, MN: Liturgical Press, 1990).

Herbert Vorgrimler, *Sacramental Theology* (Collegeville, MN: Liturgical Press, 1992).

James F. White, *Sacraments in Protestant Practice and Faith* (Nashville, TN: Abingdon Press, 1999).

Edward Yarnold, *The Awe-Inspiring Rites of Initiation: Origins of the RCIA* (Collegeville, MN: Liturgical Press, 1994).

7

Liturgy and the Fullness of Life: Liturgical Spirituality

How does worship shape Christian living?
Are capacities for praise and lament related?
In what sense does worship make people 'normal' before God?

Perhaps because so much liturgical study has been preoccupied with texts and their historical development, questions about the spirituality of Christian worship have sometimes been neglected. For example, Ann Loades notes how difficult it is, in looking into the literature produced in liturgical studies, to answer the question 'Why worship?'[1] The question may not be as simple as it might at first seem, but nevertheless, that reflection on such matters is at best marginal in much liturgical study is a shame, especially given that 'spirituality' is apparently more and more important to more and more people in our contemporary cultural context. The spirituality of the liturgy seems to be an increasingly pressing matter for liturgical studies to address, and at least attempting to articulate a liturgical spirituality seems encumbent on those presently engaged in liturgical study, particularly if they hope or claim that their work will serve the mission of the church. Hence, this chapter explores some basic features of liturgical spirituality and asks what worship might have to do with the fullness of life.

Worship as Response

Contemporary theologians who have approached the question 'Why worship?' have proposed different kinds of answers. A widely expressed belief is that worship is primarily about human response to the prior expression of divine grace towards creaturely need. For example, in the opening essay in the ecumenical collection *The Study of Liturgy*, J. D. Critchton writes that 'because it is God who always takes the initiative, Christian worship is best discussed in terms of response',[2] or as Ann Loades puts the point, 'Christian human beings engage with . . . God, or seek to do so because they believe . . . God seeks them'.[3] Crichton insists that 'if this is so, worship must be seen in the context of saving history, which is the record of divine initiative',[4] and Loades particularly relates Christian worship to the core Christian doctrine of the incarnation. Of the mystery of gracious, divine initiative, she speaks of 'God's marvellous ambiguity – not just his flesh-making but his flesh-taking', which 'means that the unsayable God becomes Word made flesh – to some degree sayable in his seeking', and this as 'some reason for worship'.[5]

And the heart of the human response is thanks and praise. Daniel Hardy and David Ford reflect on the nature of praise: they speak of the 'strange logic' of praise 'perfecting perfection' and of thanks 'completing the completed'.[6] In perfecting perfection, praise is 'an attempt to cope with the abundance of God's love',[7] 'an enhancement of what is already valued' which is marked by free and generous response:

> When we find something of quality and express our appreciation, that very expression adds something to the situation. This is even more so in the case of praise of a person. To recognise worth and to respond to it with praise is to create a new relationship. This new mutual delight is itself something of worth, an enhancement of what is already valued.
>
> There need be no end to this: there can be an infinite spiral of free response and expression of it in look or word or act. Like lovers writing letters or just looking into each other's eyes, the expression of appreciation is not an optional extra in the relationship; it is intrinsic to its quality, and is also a measure of all behaviour within it.[8]

Thanks is the companion of praise, 'completing what is completed': 'When something has happened that is good then thanks is one way (and perhaps the most fully personal way) for that to overflow into the present and the future.'[9]

Elsewhere, David Ford writes with another colleague to speak of the possibility of 'praising open' the future: 'Praise opens up the horizon within which present conditions can be seen to contradict the life and will of God; it energizes commitment to a new and different future; and it helps set an agenda for change'.[10] In these accounts, both thanks and praise hold great potential to yield a fuller life.

It is, however, by no means the case that the liturgy expresses only joyful emotion, as will be recalled in relation to our discussion of the psalms in Chapter 3. One feature of a number of recent liturgies is the expression of lament. The service 'Facing Pain' in *New Patterns for Worship* is one such example,[11] and a number of ecumenical and interfaith liturgies have been published by Frank Henderson.[12] Henderson's *Liturgies of Lament* includes provision for, among other things, liturgies commemorating the Holocaust, which has also been a focus of Michael Downey's reflection on the relationship between worship and spirituality. One of Downey's most challenging contributions is to relate this sample of a Holocaust anthology by Yaffa Eliach:

> In 'The First Hanukkah Light in Bergen Belsen' she recounts how the victims construct a makeshift hanukkiah from a wooden clog, strings, and shoe polish to serve as oil. Not far from the heaps of bodies, the living skeletons assemble to participate in the kindling of Hanukkah lights. Aware of the heap of the dead and the assembly of living skeletons, the rabbi hesitates and then proceeds with the third blessing – in which God, addressed as Lord and King of the Universe, is blessed for keeping, preserving, and enabling the people of the covenant to reach this season. When questioned as to why (under such circumstances) he would address God in such terms, the rabbi explains that the large crowd of living Jews, their faces expressing faith, devotion, and concentration as they listen to the rite, provides the justification for that kind of prayer. According to the rabbi ... in times like this, when during the lighting of the Hanukkah lights they see in front

of them the heaps of bodies of their beloved fathers, mothers, brothers, sisters, sons, and daughters, and death is looking from every corner, then the rabbi has grounds for reciting the third blessing in praise of God's goodness and providence.[13]

This, as Ann Loades affirms, is a powerful response to the question 'Why worship?'

The Holocaust is also a focus of David Power's insistence that Christian liturgy must include lament, an expression of which is his eucharistic prayer:

We thank you, O God, whatever our trembling, because when we are laid low, we find you in our midst, in the one on whom the Spirit descended, on whom your strong right hand has rested. We praise you for Jesus Christ, for he is the one in whose suffering your judgment speaks and in whose fire we are baptized. In him we have been promised another rule, a compassionate presence, even amid strife and suffering and in hours of darkness . . .[14]

As well as enlarging the place of lament, some contemporary liturgies also make space for honest expression of doubt alongside or instead of use of inherited creeds. For example, at Philadelphia Cathedral, Richard Giles has developed a seasonal collection of simple scripture juxtapositions, the latter of which is always Mark 9.23, 'Lord, I believe, help my unbelief'.[15] In Britain, a particularly striking honest affirmation, in a credal style, is that found in the Northumbria Community's resources for daily prayer:

Lord, you have always given bread for the coming day,
And though I am poor, today I believe.
Lord, you have always given strength for the coming day,
And though I am weak, today I believe.
Lord, you have always given peace for the coming day,
And though of anxious heart, today I believe . . .[16]

After several more statements of this kind, the Northumbria affirmation ends with a statement of trust in God's word, even in the face of apparent divine silence.

In these various forms, lament and praise are found adjacent to one another, or intertwined, in liturgical expression. The recovery of lament, and its links with praise, might properly be seen as informed by scripture, and one particularly powerful manifestation of this is found in the Kenyan *Our Modern Service*, where a classic scripture portion on lament, Habukkuk 3.17–18, is adjusted to context and contemporary circumstance:

> Though the mango tree does not blossom,
> nor the fruit be on the vines,
> the crop of the coconut fails,
> and the fields yield no food,
> the flock be cut off from the fold,
> and there be no herd in the stall,
> yet I will rejoice in the Lord,
> I will be joyful in the God of my salvation.
> Glory to the Father, to the Son, and to the Holy Spirit . . .[17]

Liturgy Shaping Life

The whole liturgy may be seen as response to God, with each part of it shaping the spirituality of those who engage. The different parts of Christian worship can be seen as holding out transforming means of grace: praise, which is about the other-centredness essential to being saved; attention to scripture, which can lead to solidarity with others in different times and places, with all that there is to be learned from their stories; confession, which allows for pathways through shame and guilt to reconciliation; intercession, which can nurture compassion; eucharist, which can earth gratitude, and so on. In these ways, worship can be seen as offering resources to grasp a life of beatitude, or in Aidan Kavanagh's more loaded talk, to be 'normalized' before God.

Kavanagh confidently asserts that what human beings need to be made whole is embedded in the basic aspects of liturgy, and that in engaging in the liturgy, worshippers can be enabled to recognize the 'frenzy of the abnormal'[18] in the world around them, in which praise, reconciliation, compassion, gratitude and so on may be sharply lacking. For Kavanagh, orthodox

Christian liturgy (and orthodox means 'right worship') 'is about nothing less than ultimate, rather than immediate, survival. It is about life forever by grace and promise'[19] and in focusing on divine gifts that foster human flourishing it 'play[s] extremely hard ball with the world by remaining constantly clear-headed about what the world cannot do for itself, and about its perennial need for grace and judgment'.[20] It 'steadily regards the world as abnormal by own choice'. Positively put the liturgy celebrates and witnesses to the good things that God gives for human flourishing. In celebrating liturgy, in being shaped by its patterns, imbibing its dynamics, and absorbing its resources of gratitude, etc., the church may, Kavanagh hopes, show the world what it is for the world to 'actively co-operat[e] with God in its own rehabilitation'.[21] It opens up 'the world rendered normal' through communion with God, 'to do . . . the world as the world issues constantly from God's creating and redeeming hand'.[22]

We find in a Kavanagh's vision a great onus on the church to be inviting, but also to challenge: for liturgy should disconcert the world, surge against, 'upend and subvert' the abnormality of disordered creation, and 'this is a frightful ministry carried on with trembling hands and a dry mouth, for the world stops being cute when told it is morbid'.[23] Kavanagh's thinking certainly offers a serious contribution from liturgy to contemporary debates about the mission of the church.

Indeed, a recent important collection of essays by a range of Lutheran theologians develops the kind of thinking that Kavanagh advances, though with a perhaps more practical bent. Their collective point is that worship turns the Christian people 'inside out':

Lines of connection and meaning run out from the worship gathering to the very contours of ordinary life, to the structures of our societies, to the commerce and communication between peoples, to the earth itself and all its animate and inanimate inhabitants. The stories of Christian worship tell of the hope and life, passion and loss, sin, need and death that all people know. And they narrate the judgement and passion of God amid this universal need, proclaiming God's still unfrustrated, continuing creation of all things and God's triumphant, all-covering mercy.

If the emphasis here is on the word, it also turns to sacrament:

> Furthermore, the meal of Christian worship promises a time when there will be food for all. And the bath, which has introduced each of us to participation in Christian worship, identifies the baptized with Jesus Christ, who identifies with all. Even in its most personal moments – my baptism, a Bible story I love, the body and blood of Christ given and shed for me – Christian worship always refers to the wider world. Baptism makes me brother or sister of a multitude. The Bible story draws the earth itself into its saving narrative. The food of communion is always 'given and shed' for a plural 'you' and is passed on and on to the hungry world.[24]

For these Lutherans, what is so significant for mission in contemporary culture is the capacity of worship to stretch beyond any individual concerns and to embrace the wider world and its peoples. The point is put attractively in this challenge:

> If you are accustomed to pray using something like the words of the old Sunday school song – 'into my heart, into my heart, come into my heart, Lord Jesus; come in today; come in to stay; come into my heart, Lord Jesus' – be careful. He will come, as he promises. But when he comes, he will bring with him all those who belong to him. That is a great crowd. If it is truly Christ who comes, your heart will be filled with all the little and needy ones of the earth.[25]

Fundamental here is that the centrality of Christ enables openness to others, a point that must somehow be reconciled with the sense that liturgy also powerfully challenges the world.

Meditating, perhaps, between an accent on openness and challenge is Robert Hovda, who writes with a strong vision of worship potentially 'creating a kingdom scene'.[26] Throughout his work, Hovda is absolutely consistent in his belief that worship can facilitate experience that reveals to those who participate a sense of God's reign. His conviction is that 'what is most important about public worship is that we gather the sisters and brothers together for a festival, a celebration of the reign of God (not yet terribly evident in daily life nor in the institutions of society), that helps us feel so good about ourselves, so important, so dignified, so precious, so free, so much at one.'[27]

Despite the rosy prose, he is careful to distinguish such festivity from either self-indulgence or escapism, and he clearly wants the sense of God's reign that such festivity may yield to contest what it judges to be impoverished and diminutive of human life. So, at its best,

> liturgical celebration, like a parable, takes us by the hairs of our heads, lifts us momentarily out of the cesspool of injustice we call home, puts us in the promised and challenging reign of God, where all are treated like we have never been treated anywhere else . . . where we are bowed to and sprinkled and censed and kissed and touched and where we share equally among all a holy food and drink.[28]

Worship, for Hovda, through a complex interplay of things said and done may invite imaginative participation in an alternative 'world'. To quote from Hovda again, the experience of these things may 'relax the tight grip of the status quo, so that people can move and breathe and envision alternatives' to the ways in which they are living.[29]

Don Sailers directly echoes Hovda's vision of liturgy as an arena for discernment of God's reign when he cites with approval a story of a minister and member of a congregation conversing about liturgy's work and purpose. As a means of describing the potential of good celebration to allow for personal and communal change, the minister suggests that 'it's like a dream . . . a vision . . . that people gather for prayer, worshiping, offering praise, thanksgiving, the music, the responding, singing. At some point [the people may] say "we could stay here forever". That's the kingdom.'[30] For Saliers, like Hovda, 'good liturgy disturbs, breaks open, and discloses a new world'.[31] And Saliers supplies some anecdotes about his personal sense of the kind of luminous moments that may surrender the grace of new order: for instance, he relates a conversation with a child who liked to sing a particular hymn because 'it's words taste so good'; he reflects on a service of baptismal renewal in which he shared after which the presider asked him 'was that a sacrament or a revival . . .? I couldn't tell the difference';[32] he writes of adding his own voice to the Exsultet of Easter as it was proclaimed by people from many different nations 'in several languages . . . as though the whole world had gathered in one place'.[33]

Links between Liturgy and Life

Ron Anderson identifies some links between liturgy and life as an alternative way of approaching the spirituality of the liturgy. He focuses on baptismal renunciation of sin and profession of faith; corporate confession of sin; intercession; and eucharistic prayer. Of the baptismal renunciations, Anderson writes:

> when I read the newspaper headlines each morning, with stories of children or parents killing children, and declining initial age of involvement in drug use, and the country's increasing disgust with, yet complacency about, the lack of moral character in our leaders, I wonder how can we *not* ask these questions.[34]

The questions posed to candidates for baptism are about the kinds of daily choices – both large and small – that confront all of us, for example, 'How will I respond to the trouble I see in the world?' Such questions, Anderson suggests, might form good questions at the start of daily devotions, granting persons new power to speak and act in fulfilment of their vocation to love self and neighbour, but also to name experiences 'for what they were' – patterns of wickedness, injustice, and evil as well as grace and love – and to name an alternative way of being in the world. Here is a practice of which Aidan Kavanagh might approve.

Other aspects of liturgy on which Anderson focuses are weekly or regular aspects of worship. He speaks of the corporate confession of sin in liturgy as a personal and ongoing counterpart to the baptismal questions' interrogation about basic orientation in the world. Anderson counsels use of good silence to allow worshippers to review their recent experience. He sees the sequence involving corporate spoken prayer and silent personal reflection and then corporate forgiveness as a way in which the liturgy allows worshippers to integrate their experience of Sunday and that of other days of the week.[35]

To share in intercession in the Sunday assembly is to share in moments in which the links between Sunday and other experiences of the week might be especially close. Here, again, silence is important, allowing worshippers to 'hold before God' the people and concerns of recent experience. Intercession not only, in Saliers' words, 'look[s] in the direction where God's love is looking',[36] but teaches a 'moral intentionality'[37] towards the world and its diverse people in various states of the human condition. Inherited forms of prayer, such as responsorial litanies, can be seen as means that teach wide-ranging attention to those in need, who need not just sentiment but solidarity. Space for intercession is very often a particularly strong feature of worship in mainstream or old-line traditions, and is sometimes oddly lacking in some of the newer traditions. One exception is the practice of 'Tonsung Kido' ('praying aloud'), a distinctive feature of new Korean churches, in which the entire assembly may vocalize intercession simultaneously, in response to a bidding by a prayer leader. The practice has been incorporated into some denominational resources.[38] Whatever the form, Anderson counsels two essential characteristics of such prayer: first that it involves the congregation, for here it may be especially important that the liturgy is the 'people's work'; and second, following Saliers' stress on the moral intentionality that intercession invites, that petitions are linked with intent and aspiration: 'for each thing we ask of God, the intent is our action in the world in God's name and power'.[39]

Finally, Anderson turns to the great thanksgiving around the holy table. This is the church's primary opportunity to embody the scripture: 'present your bodies as a living sacrifice, holy and acceptable to God, which is your spiritual worship' (Rom. 12.1). To focus on the context of eucharistic prayer is, however, by no means to restrict the relevance of Paul's call, to draw back from the challenge to give worth to God in the whole of life. As with intercession, intent is all important: it is 'the whole of our broken lives, the whole of our imperfect selves, that we offer to God for transformation'.[40] Anderson's suggestion is that participation in eucharistic prayer and eucharistic sharing can teach a way to yield life to God: 'what we receive at the Table is but the model for the community gathered about each table at home and workplace, day in and day out – until the next Lord's day and until the Lord comes'.[41]

Conclusion: Sacramental Spirituality

Anderson's last point here brings us to what many might regard as the heart of a sacramental spirituality, and to close this chapter, we consider two perspectives – one ancient, one contemporary – on what this might mean. Augustine, in one of his most famous sermons, told his listeners that if they wished to understand the body of Christ, then they ought to turn to the text of 1 Corinthians 12.27: 'you are the body of Christ, and his members'. At the eucharist, he told them, they were to 'be what you see, become what you are'.

The contemporary theologian Don Saliers affirms Augustine's call. He writes of the purpose of the Christian people being to embody the eucharistic action of 'taking, blessing, breaking and giving' bread and wine. The action of which the church both remembers and joins Jesus in eucharistic celebration is itself a pattern for Christian spirituality, and we encounter grace in living in the way the celebration unfolds: just as bread and wine are taken, we are to offer ourselves into God's hands, to give ourselves to God's purposes. Just as thanksgiving is raised up, we are to 'live the thanksgiving', in gratitude for the mighty acts of God that eucharistic prayer narrates, 'leaning into' its proclamation. Just as bread is broken and wine poured out, we must be vulnerable to all faith demands. And just as nourishment is shared, so we 'must be prepared to be given for others'. [42] According to Saliers, this is the heart of the dynamic of eucharist: 'Grace is given in the eucharist, but this is the grace we also encounter in offering, blessing, breaking open, and sharing our lives with all in this needy world.'[43] In this, we see that liturgical spirituality is closely connected with mission.

Further Reading

Byron Anderson, *Worship and Christian Identity: Practicing Ourselves* (Collegeville, MN: Liturgical Press, 2003).

David Brown and Ann Loades (eds), *The Sense of the Sacramental: Movement and Measure in Art and Music, Time and Place* (London: SPCK, 1995).

Michael Downey, *Worship at the Margins: Liturgy and Spirituality* (Washington, DC: Pastoral Press, 1991).

Daniel W. Hardy and David F. Ford, *Jubilate: Theology in Praise* (London: Darton, Longman and Todd, 1984).

Aidan Kavanagh, *On Liturgical Theology* (Collegeville, MN: Liturgical Press, 1984).

Philip Pfatteicher, *Liturgical Spirituality* (Valley Forge, PA: Trinity Press International, 1997).

Don E. Saliers, *Worship and Spirituality* (Akron, OH: Order of St Luke, 1996).

Don E. Saliers, *Worship Come to Its Senses* (Nashville, TN: Abingdon, 1996).

Geoffrey Wainwright, Doxology: *The Praise of God in Worship, Doctrine and Life* (Akron, OH: Order of St Luke, 2000).

Susan J. White, *The Spirit of Worship: The Liturgical Tradition* (London: Darton, Longman and Todd, 2000).

Conclusion: Presiding in Liturgy

What is most important for presiders in worship?
How important is catechesis on liturgy?
Why change patterns of worship?

The English word 'presider' comes from the Latin for 'sit before', and is presently the most common ecumenical term for the one who leads the Christian people in worship.

Everything in the preceding chapters of this book is relevant to the art of presiding in liturgy, to negotiating the tensions of 'sitting before' others in worship. Presiders need to be clear about the priority of participation, sensitive to many possible modes of participation and alert to diverse ways in which members of the congregations they seek to serve might actually be engaging in liturgy. The people for whom they are presiding may share 'official', denominational interpretations of their worship practices, or may, in some way, be 'praying between the lines', as just two among many possibilities. Presiders need to be wise about how liturgical meaning engages much more than texts alone (Introduction).

Presiders are also well-served by awareness of the long tradition which informs wide contemporary consensus, as well as inspires and legitimizes rich diversity. At the very least, familiarity with the tradition can yield important resources for shaping worship in ways that share dynamics with liturgies prayed by forebears in the faith as they gathered before God, as well as express commonalities with countless other assemblies dispersed throughout the contemporary world. And word and sacrament, the heart of the tradition, are not only durable and defining characteristics of Christian worship (Chapter 1) but, if they are means of God's self-giving, also give shape to the mission of God in which Christians are beckoned to share.

Still, it is not enough only to be delighted by word and sacrament. Presiders also need to be wise to ways the space and symbols they freely choose – or which they inherit – interact with what is central in the liturgical tradition. They need to develop visual theologies in their own persons, apart from in those spaces in which they assume the role of host (Chapter 2). And the range of music presiders encourage or inhibit in assemblies has very important implications for the hospitality of the occasions they serve. Therefore, presiders need a strong vision of what music can do to make people feel welcome, or on edge, as might variously be appropriate (Chapter 3). Likewise, they need to find ways to enable the assembly to engage with the comfort and challenge of scripture; to hear, speak and enact transforming words (Chapter 4). In each of these ways, presiders embrace major responsibilities for shaping Christian worship, and for shaping Christian worshippers.

In these things, they also give shape to the mission of the church, stretching into or shrinking from its challenges. Justin Martyr (Chapter 1) associates the presider with guardianship – particularly, for Justin, guardianship of the poor, although by extention the sense is that the presider's work is to protect a kind of inclusivity. Inclusivity is both demanding and complex, but no one more than presiders are privileged to demonstrate and teach it in the community of the church (Chapter 5). No less are they privileged to touch others in the tender moments of their lives' transitions and to bless them in their strengths as they share with them in the celebration of sacraments. However, in addition to these ways of being alongside others, presidency also invites leaders to summon Christian communities to robust engagement with, sometimes challenge to, their surrounding cultures in ways that reflect the vigour of the evangelistic reasons for the development of the liturgical seasons (Chapter 6). Furthermore, the richness and rootedness of the assembly's spirituality (Chapter 7) may depend upon presiders' ministry. The fullness of life may be lost or found because of who and how they are before others.

The art of presidency requires careful reflection.

Strong, Loving and Wise

When William Seth Adams reflects on presidency, he identifies two related dynamics for which presiders have particular responsibility: 'expression' and 'impression': 'In our rituals, the church *expresses* itself and in our rituals the church *impresses* itself back on itself. In what we do and say, we express what we believe and what we believe is impressed back upon us'.[1] Presiders guide these two related processes. At least two kinds of catechesis and teaching about liturgy are essential to effect this dual movement: first, teaching for presiders themselves, and second teaching that presiders are able to offer to others to nurture their participation. As *Sacrosanctum concilium* asserts, presiders 'must realize that when the liturgy is celebrated something more is required than the mere observance of the laws governing valid and lawful celebration; it is also their duty to ensure that the faithful take part fully aware of what they are doing, actively engaged in the rite, and enriched by its effects'.[2]

In considering what presiders really need and need to know, Robert Hovda speaks of the essential qualification of presidency being 'depth and commitment of faith', comprised of 'feelings of awe, mystery, the holy, reverence, which simply have to be present in one who presides in liturgical celebration . . . The best of presiding techniques appear shrill, pretentious, self-assertive and empty without this qualification. The worst techniques are made bearable (if not delectable) by its presence'.[3] He suggests that sitting before others must be done winsomely. But, as well as attracting, presiding is not without an element of challenge. It may involve, among other things, sometimes changing the way people pray.

Reflecting on his four decades of involvement in liturgical renewal, James White acknowledges that the liturgist's task to sometimes change people's prayer disturbs him, but nevertheless identifies four key justifiable reasons for doing so: first, liturgical prayer must change if it is necessary to reflect 'more accurately the true nature of God and God's relation to humans. For example, prayer addressed to God as the purveyor of success needs change'. Second, the liturgy 'must be made to reflect and teach justice, though it ought not preach. Prayers in former wedding services, which prayed that the woman

alone "fortify herself against weakness", certainly need replacing'. Third, liturgical language must be 'made accessible to all, not just to those who understand what it is to be "sore let and hindered". "Plight thee my troth" always
made me think of how we feed hogs, hardly what Cranmer intended!' Fourth
and finally, 'the way we pray has to be shaped to relate to the prayer of all
Christians. Christian prayer demands the company of many voices, present
or unseen. We proclaim the same story and implore God's continuance of the
same work'.[4] Especially if ordained, the presider can never simply be allied
with the local congregation but is a living reminder of the church's catholic-
ity, its wide resources, its long memory, its rich treasure store, bigger than any
particular community's hold on it. This has an unavoidable dimension of
challenge about it: the presider is called to transcend the local church and is
there to resource it to transcend its preferences, its prejudices, its wants, and
certainly its *felt* needs.

Where presidency is perceived in this way, there is an inevitable potential
for conflict in presiders' ministries, however much their main focus ought to
be encouragement. Engagement in the renewal of worship means, at least at
times, pushing for change (certainly never avoiding change), and knowing
when to make the push. This does not necessarily mean waiting for consensus, but rather nurturing change in appropriate ways. James Empereur
writes:

> It is important to find out who is actually praying in the parish and then
> enlist them in forming communities. In one sense it is still meaningful to
> work with the people who wish to be ministered to. Those who want to
> go their own way will survive on their own or will disassociate, which may
> be preferable. The question should never be: But are the people ready for
> this? But rather: Are there some who are ready? The whole church is never
> moved at the same rate in every place.[5]

And some sort of engagement in some sort of renewal should always be
possible. If it seems difficult, perhaps 'if you cannot find apostolically committed people in your parish, . . . you are not looking in the correct place'.
And if, at the end of searching, 'your parish is nearly one hundred percent
uncommitted, it should die. It is a countersign'.[6] Similarly clear-eyed is

Richard Giles, who emphasizes that ordination is a commission to 'take care of that and those entrusted to us'. But

> Those charged to 'take care' very easily become those who merely 'care take' (i.e. who serve as janitors for the people of God). Missionaries and prophets, and those willing to shake up the local church for the sake of the Kingdom of God, are in short supply in our ranks. Indeed the unforgivable sin for clergy is still considered to be that of losing someone from the congregation, whereas a parting of the ways may be the first step in the renewal of congregational life.[7]

Perhaps, though, the main thing about which presiders must remain clear-eyed is their own work of enabling others' participation. Everything about presidency finds its context in the participation of the assembly. The congregation is not an audience, and there is no presidency apart from widespread participation, for without such participation, leadership transmutes into something else – domination not orchestration of the assembly. From his Catholic context, James Empereur suggests a key guideline that has relevance across the traditions: 'The general principle that the priest should not do anything that others can do is a good working principle if it is properly understood. If it reduces the priest to a mere sacramental functionary, then ultimately this principle is counterproductive'.[8]

None of the above tasks will be performed without making mistakes. John Hughes writes bravely and movingly of a number of occasions on which liturgical leaders admitted their misjudgements. On one such occasion, on a Good Friday, the leaders set a large cross alongside the reading of verses from Isaiah 53 – 'Surely he took up our infirmities and carried our sorrows . . . he was pierced for our transgressions, he was crushed for our iniquities' (vv. 4–5) – and then:

> In a time of reflection, I encouraged people to write down the things they wanted to nail to the cross, and then to bring their pieces of paper to the cross and hammer them in, symbolizing a 'letting go'. It was very moving to see a hundred or more people queuing to hammer their burdens to the cross. On the centrepiece one member had written, 'I hate the church'.

This opportunity provided a start to fresh beginnings. On another occasion, following preaching on the shepherding imagery of Ezekiel 34, as a way of providing a means of responding to the word the leaders 'decided to ask the people's forgiveness for those occasions when we or our predecessors had abused our leadership authority'.

To symbolize this I went into the congregation with a shepherd's staff, asking forgiveness for times when we and other leaders might have abused our spiritual authority. We then held several shepherd's staffs at the sanctuary steps, while people could come up and kneel, holding the staff and then choosing to let it go when they were ready, symbolizing forgiveness and letting go of a past conflict. These symbolic actions allowed people to express before God the weight of the suppressed dealings they had been carrying, which hindered both them and the church. This was an important moment in our church's life. Many people came forward for prayer – some in considerable distress from past experiences – and received healing at different levels . . .[9]

In their ministry, presiders must be 'strong, loving and wise', to cite the title of perhaps the most impressive text on presidential responsibilities, Robert Hovda's text of that name. Above all, Hovda stresses the presider's vision: 'to make [liturgy] experiential today for all of us . . . to take that frequently dreadful and *pro forma* Sunday Eucharistic assembly and do it so attractively, so dazzlingly, that it grabs our insides'.[10]

To close the book, here are two of my own experiences of liturgy 'grabbing the insides' to serve as an invitation to readers to think of and foster such experience in their own worshipping communities. The first of my examples followed the reading of the first verses of Romans 5, which speaks of the dynamic of a faith in which suffering produces endurance, endurance produces character, character produces hope, and so on. Paul ascribes this dynamic to the believer's assurance of justification and to the indwelling presence of the Holy Spirit. The reading is given in the lectionary for proclamation on the day of Pentecost and I heard the reading, on this occasion, in the context of a Pentecost liturgy. It was the custom of the congregation I was visiting for members of the assembly to respond to the reading by sharing personal reflections before attention turned to the next scripture reading on the way to the sermon. I recall one woman standing to speak about Romans 5. She had, she revealed, just undergone a programme of chemotherapy. And she observed that 'so often in this world, suffering leads to bitterness and bitterness to isolation, but it does not have to be this way. For in these days, I have discovered that suffering may lead to endurance and endurance to hope'. This incident is not only the strongest possible advocate for the merit of 'dialogical' approaches to the sermon (see Chapter 4), if it was not a 'kingdom scene' (Chapter 7), I can hardly imagine what is!

Similarly, on another occasion, I recall a woman, who apparently new to the experience of worship, stood to give testimony: 'Tonight, in this service, I have realized that I can be beautiful, even in my own eyes.'[11]

Notes

Introduction Participating in Liturgy

1 Antonio Skarmeta, *Il Postino* (ET London: Bloomsbury, 1996), p. 37.
2 Skarmeta, *Il Postino*, p. 86.
3 *Methodist Worship Book* (Peterborough: Methodist Publishing House, 1999), p. viii.
4 *New Patterns for Worship* (London: Church House Publishing, 2002), p. 1; compare *Common Worship* (London: Church House Publishing, 2000): 'worship is more than what is said: it is also what is done and how it is done' (p. x).
5 And so the respected liturgist James White writes: 'I like to speak of Christian worship as speaking and touching in Christ's name', James F. White, 'Coming Together in Christ's Name', Blair Gilmore-Meeks (ed.), *The Landscape of Praise: Readings in Liturgical Renewal* (Valley Forge, PA: Trinity Press International, 1997), pp. 152–6, hinting at the multisensual dimensions of worship.
6 Robert Hovda, 'Response to the Berakah Award', John F. Baldovin (ed.), *Robert Hovda: The Amen Corner* (Collegeville, MN: Liturgical Press, 1994), pp. 241–53.
7 Susan J. White, *Christian Worship and Technological Change* (Nashville, TN: Abingdon, 1994) explores some of these issues in more detail.
8 *Sacrosanctum concilium* 14. Austin Flannery (ed.), *Vatican Council II: Conciliar and Post-Conciliar Documents* (New York: Costello, 1977).
9 Don E. Saliers, 'Christian Spirituality in an Ecumenical Age', Louis Dupré and Don E. Saliers (eds), *Christian Spirituality III: Post-Reformation and Modern* (London: SCM Press, 1989), pp. 520–44; cf. Don E. Saliers, 'The Nature of Worship: Community Lived in Praise of God', Robin Leaver and James Litton (eds), *Duty and Delight: Routley Remembered* (Norwich: Canterbury Press, 1985), pp. 35–45: 'nothing has symbolized more dramatically this "age of liturgical reform" than the Second Vatican Council', p. 38.

10 Gordon W. Lathrop, 'Strong Center, Open Door: A Vision of Continuing Liturgical Renewal', *Worship* 75 (2001), pp. 35–45.

11 *Methodist Worship Book*, p. vii.

12 *Common Worship*, p. ix.

13 *Worship from the United Reformed Church*, 'Introduction to Communion Orders', first page (no page number).

14 L. Edward Phillips, 'Whose Worship is it Anyway?', E. Byron Anderson (ed.) *Worship Matters: A United Methodist Guide to Ways of Worship*, Volume I (Nashville, TN: Discipleship Resources, 1999), pp. 80–5.

15 Gabe Huck, 'The Very Nature of the Liturgy', Kathleen Hughes (ed.), *Finding Voice to Give God Praise: Essays on the Many Languages of the Liturgy* (Collegeville, MN: Liturgical Press, 1998), pp. 299–309.

16 Huck, 'The Very Nature', p. 299.

17 James F. White, 'Forum: Some Lessons in Liturgical Pedagogy', *Worship* 68 (1994), pp. 438–50.

18 David N. Power, *Worship: Culture and Theology* (Washington, DC: Pastoral Press, 1990), p. 276.

19 Marjorie Procter-Smith, *Praying with Our Eyes Open: Engendering Feminist Liturgical Prayer* (Nashville, TN: Abingdon Press, 1995), pp. 31–3.

Chapter 1 Scripture and Sacrament

1 Justin Martyr, *1 Apology* 67; this translation from Gordon Lathrop, *Holy Things: A Liturgical Theology* (Minneapolis, MN: Fortress Press, 1993), pp. 31–2.

2 Cited here from James Schellen, 'The Revised Sacramentary: Revisiting the Eucharistic Renewal of Vatican II', Kathleen Hughes (ed.), *Finding Voice to Give God Praise: Essays in the Many Languages of the Liturgy* (Collegeville, MN: Liturgical Press, 1998), pp. 257–8.

3 *Methodist Worship Book* (Peterborough: Methodist Publishing House, 1999), pp. 221–2.

4 Cited here from Thomas Best and Dagmar Heller (eds), *Eucharistic Worship in Ecumenical Contexts: The Lima Liturgy – and Beyond* (Geneva: WCC Publications, 1995), p. 35.

5 *Sacrosanctum concilium* 53. Austin Flannery (ed.), *Vatican Council II: Conciliar and Post-Conciliar Documents* (New York: Costello, 1977).

6 *Worship from the United Reformed Church* (London: United Reformed Church, 2003), p. 6.

7 *Worship from the United Reformed Church*, p. 21.

8 An example of Reformed reserve with aspects of the lectionary can be found in John Goldingay (interestingly, an Anglican!), 'Canon and Lection', Bryan Spinks and Iain Torrance (eds), *To Glorify God: Essays on Modern Reformed Liturgy* (Edinburgh: T & T Clark, 1999), pp. 85–97.

9 *Common Worship* (London: Church House Publishing, 2000), p. 332.

10 *Common Worship*, p. 540.

11 *Common Worship*, p. 540.

12 *New Patterns for Worship* (London: Church House Publishing, 2002), pp. 98–122.

13 *New Patterns for Worship*, p. 106.

14 See Gordon W. Lathrop, *What Are the Essentials of Christian Worship?* (Minneapolis, MN: Fortress Press, 1996), volume I of the 'Open Questions in Worship' series, which represents one of the most recent and best expressions of this consensus, appropriating it for the North American Lutheran tradition.

15 See Ronald Jasper and Geoffrey Cumming (eds), *Prayers of the Eucharist: Early and Reformed* (Collegeville, MN: Liturgical Press, third edition, 1987), pp. 31–8. For recent critique of Vatican II's liturgical reform, and particularly the reliance of its crafters on the Hippolytan construct, see Catherine Pickstock, *After Writing: The Liturgical Consummation of History* (Oxford: Blackwell, 1998), pp. 171–5; also, David Torevell, *Losing the Sacred: Ritual, Modernity and Liturgical Reform* (Edinburgh: T & T Clark, 2000), pp. 146–69.

16 *Baptism, Eucharist and Ministry* (Geneva: World Council of Churches, 1982), and a wealth of material flowing from it.

17 Gordon Wakefield, *An Outline of Christian Worship* (Edinburgh: T & T Clark, 1998), pp. 153–4.

18 Geoffrey Wainwright, 'The Church as a Worshipping Community', *Worship with One Accord: Where Liturgy and Ecumenism Embrace* (New York: Oxford University Press, 1997), p. 30.

19 The (American) *United Methodist Book of Worship* (Nashville, TN: United Methodist Publishing House, 1989) is a good example; a related example is *Uniting in Worship* (Melbourne: Uniting Church Press, 1988), the book of the Uniting Church of Australia (comprised of formerly Methodist and Reformed churches), which calls its communion service 'A Service of Word and Sacrament'.

20 International Commission on English in the Liturgy, Collect for the Twentieth Sunday in Ordinary Time, *Opening Prayers: Scripture-Related Collects for Years A, B and C from the Sacramentary* (Norwich: Canterbury Press, 1997), p. 94.

21 *Methodist Worship Book*, p. 26.

22 *Common Worship*, p. x.

23 David Stancliffe, *God's Pattern: Shaping Our Worship, Ministry and Life* (London: SPCK, 2003).

24 Stancliffe, *God's Pattern*, pp. 18–20.

25 Such 'gestural theology' will be a major theme of the next chapter.

26 For an engaging treatment of this ritual, see Michael Johnson, *Engaging the Word* (Cambridge, MA: Cowley, 1998), pp. 145–8.

27 Augustine, *Tractus on John*, 80.3; cited by Calvin, *Institutes* IV xiv.4.

28 The complexity of, for example, Matthew 28 as a warrant for baptism centres around the use of a *trinitarian* formula, unusual elsewhere in the Gospels, cited in a *post-resurrection* encounter. The mandate is simply beyond any obvious kind of historical verification, including those used in relation to other parts of the scriptural witness to Jesus.

29 Ignatius, *To the Romans* 7.2b; cited from Gordon Lathrop, 'The Water that Speaks: The Ordo of Baptism and its Ecumenical Implications', Thomas Best and Dagmar Heller (eds), *Becoming a Christian: The Ecumenical Implications of Our Common Baptism* (Geneva: World Council of Churches, 1999), p. 13.

30 For detailed exploration of this text, see Paul Bradshaw, Maxwell E. Johnson and L. Edward Philips, *The Apostolic Tradition: A Commentary* (Minneapolis, MN: Fortress Press, 2002).

31 Cited here from Jasper and Cumming *Prayers of the Eucharist*, pp. 34–5.

32 Jasper and Cumming, *Prayers of the Eucharist*, p. 36.

33 Jasper and Cumming, *Prayers of the Eucharist*, p. 37.

34 Jasper and Cumming, *Prayers of the Eucharist*, p. 37.

35 Jasper and Cumming, *Prayers of the Eucharist*, p. 31.

36 *Celebrate God's Presence: A Book of Services for the United Church of Canda* (Etobicoke, Ont.: United Church Publishing House, 2000), pp. 256–8; also, with slight variation, *Renewing Worship: Holy Communion and Related Rites* of the Evangelical Lutheran Church of America (Minneapolis, MN: Augsburg Press, 2004), pp. 64–5.

37 Ruth Duck, *Finding Words for Worship: A Guide for Leaders* (Louisville, KY: Westminster John Knox Press, 1995), pp. 100–1.

38 For a recent discussion, see Andrew McGowan, 'The Meals of Jesus and the Meals of the Church: Eucharistic Origins and Admission to Communion', Maxwell E. Johnson and L. Edward Philips (eds), *Studia Liturgica Diversa: Essays in Honor of Paul Bradshaw* (Portland, OR: Pastoral Press, 2004), pp. 101–16.

39 See Bruce Chilton, *A Feast of Meanings* (Leiden: Brill, 1994) and Bruce Chilton, *Jesus' Prayer and Jesus' Eucharist: His Personal Practice of Spirituality* (Valley Forge, PA: Trinity Press International, 1997).

40 N. T. Wright, *Jesus and the Victory of God* (London: SPCK, 1996), especially pp. 554–65.

41 Chilton, *Jesus' Prayer and Jesus' Eucharist*, p. 73.

Chapter 2 Space and Symbol

1 Laurence Hull Stookey, *Baptism: Christ's Act in the Church* (Nashville, TN: Abingdon Press, 1982), p. 174.

2 David Brown and Ann Loades, 'The Dance of Grace', David Brown and Ann Loades (eds), *The Sense of the Sacramental* (London: SPCK, 1995), p. 6.

3 In this chapter, I have tended to use cathedrals as my examples, emphatically not because these are the only buildings that demonstrate the points I wish to make, but because they are well-known both in Britain and abroad and so are more likely to be known by readers than less public local churches.

4 Regina Kuehn, *A Place for Baptism* (Chicago, IL: Liturgy Training Publications, 1990); Jermone Overbeck, *Ancient Fonts, Modern Lessons* (Chicago, IL: Liturgy Training Publications, 1998); Anita Stauffer, *On Baptismal Fonts: Ancient and Modern* (Nottingham: Grove Books, 1994).

5 United States Conference of Catholic Bishops, *Environment and Art in Catholic Worship* (Chicago, IL: Liturgy Training Publications, 1978) paras. 11 and 12. (This document was scripted by Robert Hovda.)

6 Richard Giles, *Re-Pitching the Tent: Re-ordering the Church Building for Worship and Mission* (Norwich: Canterbury Press, 2004).

7 Richard Giles, *Creating Uncommon Worship: Transforming the Liturgy of the Eucharist* (Norwich: Canterbury Press, 2004).

8 James F. White, *Christian Worship in North America: A Retrospective 1955–1995* (Collegeville, MN: Liturgical Press, 1997), p. 212.

9 David Stancliffe, 'Creating Sacred Space: Liturgy and Architecture Interacting', Brown and Loades (eds), *The Sense of the Sacramental* (London: SPCK, 1995), p. 58.

10 Stancliffe, 'Creating Sacred Space', p. 57.

11 Stancliffe, 'Creating Sacred Space', p. 56.

12 Bruce T. Morrill, 'The Many Bodies of Worship: Locating the Spirit's Work', Bruce T. Morrill (ed.), *Bodies of Worship: Explorations in Theory and Practice* (Collegeville, MN: Liturgical Press, 1999), p. 19.

13 Diane Karay Tripp, *Daily Prayer in the Reformed Tradition* (Cambridge: Grove Books, 1996), p. 13.

14 Daniel E. Albrecht, *Rites in the Spirit: A Ritual Approach to Pentecostal/Charismatic Worship* (Sheffield: Sheffield Academic Press, 1999).

15 Albrecht, *Rites in the Spirit*, esp. pp. 131–4, 165–70.

16 Dolores C. Williams, 'Rituals of Resistance in Womanist Worship', Marjorie Procter-Smith and Janet Walton (eds), *Women at Worship: Interpretations of*

North American Diversity (Louisville, KY: Westminster John Knox Press, 1993), pp. 216–17.

17 Don E. Saliers, *Worship as Theology: Foretaste of Glory Divine* (Nashville, TN: Abingdon Press, 1994), p. 164.

18 Saliers, *Worship as Theology*, p. 164.

19 *Odes of Solomon* 27; cited here from Edward Foley, *From Age to Age: How Christians Have Celebrated the Eucharist* (Chicago, IL: Liturgy Training Publications, 1991), p. 31.

20 Tertullian, *De corona* 3; cited here from Klemens Richter, *The Meaning of the Sacramental Symbols: Answers to Today's Questions* (Collegeville, MN: Liturgical Press, 1990), p. 132.

21 *Uniting in Worship: People's Book* (Melbourne: Uniting Church Press, 1988), pp. 32–3.

22 *Rite of Christian Initiation of Adults: Study Edition* (Chicago, IL: Liturgy Training Publications, 1988), pp. 25–6. This text has since been included in rites of Protestant traditions – such as the Evangelical Lutheran Church in America's *Renewing Worship* initiation services: *Holy Baptism and Related Services* (Minneapolis, MN: Augsburg Press, 2004).

23 Cyril of Jerusalem, *Mystagogical Catechesis*; quoted in Edward Yarnold (ed.), *The Awe-Inspiring Rites of Initiation: The Origins of the RCIA* (Collegeville, MN: Liturgical Press, 1994), pp. 83–4.

24 John K. Leonard and Nathan D. Mitchell, *The Postures of the Assembly During the Eucharistic Prayer* (Chicago, IL: Liturgy Training Publications, 1994).

25 Giles, *Creating Uncommon Worship*, pp. 163–4.

26 And because it 'is Christ' it is in the rites relating to its installation 'baptized', 'anointed' and 'clothed' as the human body might be: see Mark Boyer, *The Liturgical Environment: What the Documents Say* (Collegeville, MN: Liturgical Press, 1990), chapter: 'The Altar is Christ'.

27 *Catechism of the Catholic Church* (London: Cassell, 1994), para. 1083.

28 Gordon Lathrop, *Holy Things* (Minneapolis, MN: Fortress Press, 1993), p. 24.

29 Giles, *Creating Uncommon Worship*.

30 Gordon W. Lathrop, 'A Rebirth of Images: On the Use of the Bible in Liturgy', Dwight W. Vogel (ed.), *Primary Sources of Liturgical Theology: A Reader* (Collegeville, MN: Liturgical Press, 2000), pp. 215–24.

31 Don E. Saliers, 'Symbol in Liturgy, Liturgy as Symbol: The Domestication of Liturgical Experience', Robert J. Madden (ed.), *The Awakening Church: Twenty-Five Years of Liturgical Renewal* (Collegeville, MN: Liturgical Press, 1992), p. 75.

32 J. Michael Joncas, 'Ritual Transformations: Principles, Patterns, and Peoples', Gabe Huck (ed.), *Toward Ritual Transformation: Remembering Robert Hovda* (Collegeville, MN: Liturgical Press, 2003), pp. 49–69.

33 David N. Power, *Unsearchable Riches: Symbols in the Liturgy* (Collegeville, MN: Liturgical Press, 1984), p. 67.

34 Joseph Martos, *Doors to the Sacred: A Historical Introduction to the Sacraments of the Christian Church* (London: SCM Press, 1981), pp. 325–6.

Chapter 3 Music and Song

1 'Now the Silence' © Jaroslav J. Vadja, CopyCare 1968; cited here from *Common Ground: A Song Book for All the Churches* (Edinburgh: Saint Andrew Press, 1998).

2 Gordon Wakefield, *Methodist Spirituality* (Peterborough: Epworth Press, 1999), p. 11.

3 Gordon Wakefield, *An Outline of Christian Worship* (Edinburgh: T & T Clark, 1998), p. 138.

4 Wakefield, *An Outline of Christian Worship*, pp. 137–8.

5 E.g. Don E. Saliers, *Worship and Spirituality* (Akron, OH: Order of St Luke, 1996), p. 1; note also the subtitle of E. Byron Anderson and Bruce T. Morrill (eds), *Liturgy and the Moral Self: Humanity at Full Stretch Before God: Essays in Honor of Don E. Saliers* (Collegeville, MN: Liturgical Press, 1998).

6 Don E. Saliers, 'David's Song in Our Land', Blair Gilmer Meeks (ed.), *The Landscape of Praise: Readings in Liturgical Renewal* (Valley Forge, PA: Trinity Press International, 1997), p. 240.

7 *The Acts of St John* 94 (song: 1–6, 11b–13, 16–17, 24–32); cited here from Ron Cameron (ed.), *The Other Gospels: Non-Canonical Gospel Texts* (Philadelphia, PA: Westminster Press, 1982), pp. 91–3.

8 Saliers, 'David's Song', p. 239.

9 International Commission on English in the Liturgy, *The Psalter: A Faithful and Inclusive Rendering of the Hebrew Into Contemporary English* (Chicago, IL: Liturgy Training Publications, 1995).

10 Eugene H. Peterson, *The Message: Psalms* (Colorado Springs, CO: NavPress, 1994), p. 4.

11 Juanita Colon, *The Manhattan Psalter: The Lectio Divina of Sister Juanita Colon* (Collegeville, MN: Liturgical Press, 2002), p. 9.

12 Gabe Huck, *Liturgy with Style and Grace* (Chicago, IL: Liturgy Training Publications, 1984), p. 22.

13 United States Conference of Catholic Bishops, *Music in Catholic Worship*, para. 23; cited here from Huck, *Liturgy with Style and Grace*, p. 23.

14 Huck, *Liturgy with Style and Grace*, p. 23.

15 David F. Ford, *Self and Salvation: Being Transformed* (Cambridge: Cambridge University Press, 1999), p. 122.

16 Carol Doran and Thomas H. Troeger, *Trouble at the Table: Gathering the Tribes for Worship* (Nashville, TN: Abingdon Press, 1992), pp. 62–5.

17 John Gibson, 'Jesus, We Celebrate Your Victory' © 1987 Kingsway's Thankyou Music.

18 Brian Wren, *Praying Twice: The Music and Words of Congregational Song* (Louisville, KY: Westminster John Knox Press, 2000), pp. 210–12.

19 Pete Ward, *Growing Up Evangelical: Youthwork and the Making of a Subculture* (London: SPCK, 1996), pp. 141–2.

20 'As Newborn Stars' © Carl P. Daw, Hope Publishing Co., 1997; cited here from *Wonder, Love and Praise: A Supplement to the Hymnal 1982* (New York: Church Publishing, 1997).

21 'The Friendship and the Fear' © Matt Redman, Kingsway's Thankyou, 1997.

22 Brian Wren, *Piece Together Praise: A Theological Journey* (London: Stainer and Bell, 1996), pp. 3, 163.

23 Wren, *Praying Twice*, pp. 364–5.

Chapter 4 Discipleship and Learning: The Sermon

1 Catherine of Siena, *The Dialogue*; cited here from Gail Ramshaw, *Reviving Sacred Speech: Second Thoughts on 'Christ in Sacred Speech'* (Akron, OH: Order of St Luke, 2000), p. 29.

2 Thomas H. Troeger, *Imagining a Sermon* (Nashville, TN: Abingdon Press, 1990), pp. 42–3.

3 John Stott, *The Cross of Christ* (Leicester: IVP, 1986), p. 41.

4 David F. Ford, 'Faith in the Cities: Corinth and the Modern City', Colin E. Gunton and Daniel W. Hardy (eds), *On Being the Church: Essays on the Christian Community* (Edinburgh: T & T Clark, 1989), pp. 225–56.

5 Gail Ramshaw, *Under the Tree of Life: The Religion of a Feminist Christian* (New York: Continuum, 1998), p. 65.

6 Ramshaw, *Under the Tree of Life*, pp. 63–4.

7 E.g. Richard Giles, *Creating Uncommon Worship: Transforming the Liturgy of the Eucharist* (Norwich: Canterbury Press, 2004), pp. 127–9.

8 Discussed in more detail in the following chapter, Gordon Lathrop and Gail Ramshaw, *Readings for the Assembly* (Minneapolis, MN: Fortress Press, 1995), artfully introduces expansive language.

9 *Methodist Worship Book* (Peterborough: Methodist Publishing House, 1999), p. 222.

10 See *Common Worship*, p. 27; cf. p. 332 (note 'on occasion').

11 William Willimon, *With Glad and Generous Hearts: A Personal Look at Sunday Worship* (Nashville, TN: Upper Room, 1986), p. 94.

12 Willimon, *With Glad and Generous Hearts*, p. 98.

13 Willimon, *With Glad and Generous Hearts*, p. 94.

14 Marva Dawn, *Reaching out Without Dumbing down: A Theology of Worship for this Urgent time* (Grand Rapids: Eerdmans, 1995), pp. 205–40.

15 Dawn, *Reaching out*, p. 205.

16 Dawn, *Reaching out*, p. 240.

17 Stephen Barton, 'New Testament Interpretation as Performance', Stephen Barton, *Life Together: Family, Sexuality and Community in the New Testament and Today* (Edinburgh: T & T Clark, 2001), pp. 223–50, surveys a range of contemporary theologians who employ this metaphor.

18 Related in both: Elizabeth A. Johnson, *Friends of God and Prophets: A Feminist Theological Reading of the Communion of Saints* (London: SCM Press, 1998), pp. 167–71; and Mary Catherine Hilkert, 'Naming Grace: A Theology of Proclamation', Dwight W. Vogel (ed.), *Primary Sources of Liturgical Theology: A Reader* (Collegeville, MN: Liturgical Press, 2000), pp. 227–36.

Chapter 5 Styles and Substance: Celebrating Diversity

1 Ann Loades, 'Word and Sacrament: Recovering Integrity', Nicholas Brown (ed.), *Faith in the Public Forum* (Melbourne: Australian Theological Forum, 1999), pp. 33–4.

2 James F. White, *Protestant Worship: Traditions in Transition* (Louisville, KY: Westminster John Knox Press, 1989). The 'Frontier' tradition is a distinctively American style that has influenced other major streams in turn, the focus of chapter 7 of White's book.

3 Thomas Best and Dagmar Heller (eds), *Worship Today: Understanding, Practice and Ecumenical Implications* (Geneva: WCC Publications, 2004).

4 James F. White, *Roman Catholic Worship: From Trent to Today* (New York: Paulist Press, 1995).

5 Ronald P. Byars, *The Future of Protestant Worship: Beyond the Worship Wars* (Louisville, KY: Westminster John Knox Press, 2002), p. 17.

6 Pete Ward, *Liquid Church* (Carlisle: Paternoster Press, 2002); for a critique, see Stephen Burns, 'Mission-Shaped Worship', *Anvil: An Anglican Evangelical Journal of Theology and Mission* 22(2005) pp. 185–98.

7 To quote the title of a series of excellent short pamphlets produced by the Evangelical Lutheran Church in America, concerned to explore the phenomenon of seeker-services in the light of their inherited tradition.

8 Paul W. Pruyser, 'Narcissism in Contemporary Religion', H. Newton Maloney and Bernard Spilka (eds), *Religion in Psychodynamic Perspective: The Contributions of Paul W. Pruyser* (New York: Oxford University Press, 1991), pp. 66–82.

9 Gordon W. Lathrop, 'Liturgy and Mission in the North American Context', Thomas H. Shattauer (ed.), *Inside out: Worship in an Age of Mission* (Minneapolis, MN: Fortress Press, 1999), 201–12.

10 David F. Ford and Laurie Green, 'Distilling the Wisdom', Peter Sedgwick (ed.), *God and the City: Essays and Reflections from the Archbishop of Canterbury's Urban Theology Group* (London: Mowbray, 1995), pp. 16–24.

11 The Archbishop of Canterbury's Commission on Urban Priority Areas, *Faith in the City: A Call for Action by Church and Nation* (London: Church House Publishing, 1985), paragraph 6.110, p. 136.

12 Donald Gray, 'Postscript', Michael Perham (ed.), *Towards Liturgy* 2000 (London: SPCK, 1989), pp. 101–2.

13 E.g. *Youth-A-Part: Young People and the Church* '(London: Church House Publishing, 1996), 2.11 and 4.14.

14 *Children in the Way* (London: Church House Publishing, 1998), bishops' notes 2 and 3.

15 For detailed discussion of *New Patterns for Worship*, please see Stephen Burns, *Worship in Context: Liturgical Theology, Children and the City* (Peterborough: Epworth Press, 2006).

16 *New Patterns for Worship* (London: Church House Publishing, 2002), p. x.

17 *New Patterns*, p. 4.

18 *Patterns for Worship for the Church of England* (London: Church House Publishing, 1989), p. 5. Also, Michael Vasey, 'Promoting a Common Core', Michael Perham (ed.), *The Renewal of Common Prayer* (London: SPCK, 1993), pp. 81–101.

19 Simon Chan, *Pentecostal Theology and the Christian Spiritual Tradition* (Sheffield: Sheffield Academic Press, 2000), p. 8.

20 Gray Temple, Jr, *When God Happens* (New York: Church Publishing, 2000), pp. 37, 40–1.

21 Harvey Cox, *Fire from Heaven: The Rise of Pentecostal Spirituality and the Reshaping of Religion in the Twenty-First Century* (London: Cassell, 1996), p. 86.

22 Walter Hollenweger, *The Pentecostals*; quoted in Jean-Jacques Suurmond, *Word and Spirit at Play: Toward a Charismatic Theology* (London: SCM Press, 1994), pp. 21–2.

23 Daniel Albrecht, *Rites in the Spirit: A Ritual Approach to Pentecostal/Charismatic*

Spirituality (Sheffield: Sheffield Academic Press, 1999) – for more on which, see below; also Steven Land, *Pentecostal Spirituality: A Passion for the Kingdom* (Sheffield: Sheffield Academic Press, 1993).

24 Sue Hope poses the question: 'When will the time come when white, middle-class churches stop laughing nervously or cynically about Pentecostalism and start to listen?' Susan Hope, 'Sanctuary', Peter Sedgwick (ed.), *God in the City: Essays and Reflections from the Archbishop of Canterbury's Urban Theology Group* (London: Mowbray, 1995), pp. 191–8.

25 James Steven, *Worship in the Spirit: Charismatic Worship in the Church of England* (Carlisle: Paternoster, 2002).

26 Jonny Baker and Doug Gay with Jenny Brown, *Alternative Worship* (London: SPCK, 2003), p. xiv.

27 Baker *et al.*, *Alternative Worship*, p. xiv.

28 Baker *et al.*, *Alternative Worship*, pp. 97, 118–19.

29 Ann Morisy, *Journeying out: A New Approach to Christian Mission* (London: Continuum, 2004), p. 156. In her Glossary, Ann Maisy defines 'high symbols' as follows: 'These allude to the sacred and signify these aspects of life that can be partly known' (p. 239).

30 Morisy, *Journeying out*, p. 158.

31 Marjorie Procter-Smith, *In Her Own Rite: Constructing Feminist Liturgical Tradition* (Akron, OH: Order of St Luke, 2000), pp. 63, 66–7.

32 Janet Morley, *All Desires Known* (London: SPCK, 1992).

33 The Baptist *Gathering for Worship* includes one reference to 'Mother', in any case when allied to the more traditional parental metaphor – i.e. 'Mother and Father of us all' – as opposed to countless usages of 'Father' standing alone. *Gathering for Worship: Patterns and Prayers for the Community of Disciples* (Norwich: Canterbury Press, 2005), p. 223.

34 Ann Loades, *Searching for Lost Coins: Explorations in Christianity and Feminism* (London: SPCK, 1987).

35 *Enriching our Worship* (New York: Church Publishing, 1997); *Renewing Worship: Holy Communion and Related Rites* (Minneapolis, MN: Augsburg Press, 2004).

36 Gordon Lathrop and Gail Ramshaw, *Readings for the Assembly*, cycles A, B and C (Collegeville, MN: Liturgical Press, 1995).

37 Gabe Huck, Gordon Lathrop and Gail Ramshaw (eds), *Easter: A Sourcebook* (Chicago, IL: Liturgy Training Publications, 1992).

38 Nicola Slee, *Praying Like a Woman* (London: SPCK, 2004), pp. 140–1.

39 Rosemary Radford Ruether, *Woman-Church: Theology and Practice of Feminist Liturgical Communities* (San Francisco, CA: Harper and Row, 1985).

40 Janet Walton, *Feminist Liturgy: A Matter of Justice* (Collegeville, MN: Liturgical Press, 2000), pp. 37–8.

41 For a first attempt to do so, please see Michael Jagessar and Stephen Burns, 'Fragments of a Postcolonial Perspective on Christian Worship' forthcoming in *Worship* (2006).

42 Chrisopher Duraisingh, 'Towards a Postcolonial Re-Visioning of the Church's Faith, Witness and Communion', Ian T. Douglas and Kwok Pui-lan (eds), *Beyond Colonial Anglicanism: The Anglican Communion in the Twenty-First Century* (New York: Church Publishing, 2001), pp. 337–67.

43 R.S. Sugirtharajah, *Postcolonial Reconfigurations: A New Way of Reading the Bible and Doing Theology* (London: SCM Press, 2003), p. 4.

44 Mukti Barton, 'I am Black and Beautiful', *Black Theology: An International Journal* 2 (2004), pp. 167–87. Cf. Kwok Pui-Lan, 'The Legacy of Cultural Hegemony', Ian T. Douglas and Kwok Pui-Lan (eds), *Beyond Colonial Anglicanism*, who notes: 'The glorification of light and the denigration of darkness in the Bible and the BCP can be used to marginalize dark-skinned people and create false racial stereotypes' (p. 61).

45 Gay L. Byron, *Symbolic Blackness and Ethnic Difference in Early Christian Literature* (London: Routledge, 2002), p. 50.

46 Robert Hood, *Begrimed and Black: Christian Traditions on Black and Blackness* (London: Routledge, 1994), p. 90.

47 *Modern Services* (Nairobi: Uzima Press, 1994), p. 5.

48 Graham Kings and Geoff Morgan, *Offerings from Kenya to Anglicanism: Liturgical Texts and Contexts including 'A Kenyan Service of Holy Communion'* (Alcuin/GROW Joint Liturgical Study 50) (Cambridge: Grove Books, 2001), p. 27.

49 Two examples: Marcella Althus-Reid, *The Queer God* (London: Routledge, 2003); Robert Goss, *Queering Christ: Beyond Jesus Acted Up* (Cleveland, OH: Pilgrim Press, 2002).

50 Elizabeth Stuart, 'Exploding Mystery: Feminist Theology and the Sacramental', Beverly Clack (ed.), *Embodying Feminist Liberation Theologies* (A Special Edition of *Feminist Theology*) (London: Continuum, 2004), pp. 228–36.

51 Ann Day, 'Litany of Celebration for Open and Affirming Churches', Ruth Duck and Maren Tirabassi (eds), *Touch Holiness: Resources for Worship* (New York: Pilgrim Press, 1990), p. 219.

52 Kittridge Cherry and Zalmon O. Sherwood (eds), *Equal Rites: Lesbian and Gay Worship, Ceremonies and Celebrations* (Louisville, KY: Westminster John Knox Press, 1995).

53 Edward Gray and Scott Lee Thumma, 'Amazing, Grace! How Sweet the Sound! Southern Evangelical Religion and Gay Drag in Atlanta', Michael Clark and Robert Goss (eds), *A Rainbow of Religious Studies* (Las Colinas, TX: Monument Press, 1996), pp. 33–53.

54 International Anglican Liturgical Consultation, 'Children and Communion: An International Anglican Liturgical Consultation held in Boston, USA, 29–31 July 1985', Ruth A. Meyers (ed.), *Children at the Table: Essays on Children and the Eucharist* (New York: Church Hymnal Corporation, 1994), p. 132.

55 David Holeton, 'Welcome Children, Welcome Me', *Anglican Theological Review* 51 (1999): 93–111.

56 Elizabeth J. Smith, 'Whose Prayer Will Make the Difference? Eucharistic Renewal and Liturgical Education', David Holeton (ed.), *Our Thanks and Praise: The Eucharist in Anglicanism Today* (Toronto: Anglican Book Centre, 1998), pp. 99–114.

57 Mary Collins, 'Is the Adult Church Ready for Liturgy with Young Christians?', *Worship: Renewal to Practice* (Washington DC: Pastoral Press, 1987), pp. 277–95.

58 Collins, 'Is the Adult Church Ready . . . ?', p. 284.

59 William C. Platcher, *Narratives of a Vulnerable God: Christ, Theology and Scripture* (Louisville, KY: Westminster John Knox Press, 1993), p. 154.

60 Don E. Saliers, 'Towards a Spirituality of Inclusiveness', Nancy Eisland and Don E. Saliers (eds), *Human Disability and the Service of God: Reassessing Religious Practice* (Nashville, TN: Abingdon Press, 1998), pp. 19–31.

Chapter 6 Cycles and Crises: Time for Worship

1 The Letter of Barnabas 15.8–9; quoted in Gordon Wakefield, *An Outline of Christian Worship* (Edinburgh: T & T Clark, 1998), p. 219.

2 Dorothy C. Bass, 'Keeping Sabbath', Dorothy C. Bass (ed.), *Practicing Our Faith: A Way of Life for a Searching People* (San Francisco, CA: Jossey-Bass, 1997), pp. 75–89.

3 *Mission-Shaped Church: Church Planting and Fresh Expressions of Church in a Changing Context* (London: Church House Publishing), p. 61.

4 *Mission-Shaped Church*, p. 67.

5 Cited here from Gabe Huck and Mary Ann Simcote (eds), *A Triduum Sourcebook* (Chicago, IL: Liturgy Training Publications, 1983), pp. 74–6.

6 Cited here from Irmgard Pahl, 'The Paschal Mystery in its Central Meaning for the Shape of Christian Liturgy', *Studia Liturgica* 26 (1999), pp. 16–38.

7 Susan J. White, *A History of Women in Christian Worship* (London: SPCK, 2004), p. 13.

8 John Wilkinson, *Egeria's Travels*; cited here from Kenneth Stevenson, *Jerusalem Revisited: The Liturgical Meaning of Holy Week* (Washington, DC: Pastoral Press, 1988), pp. 57–8.

9 Quoted in Hoyt L. Hickman, Don E. Saliers, Laurence Hull Stookey and James F. White, *New Handbook of the Christian Year* (Nashville: Abingdon Press, 1992), pp. 187–9.

10 Hickman, Saliers, Stookey and White, *New Handbook of the Christian Year*, p. 190.

11 Gail Ramshaw, 'Pried Open by Prayer', E. Byron Anderson and Bruce T. Morrill (eds), *Liturgy and the Moral Self: Humanity at Full Stretch Before God: Essays in Honor of Don E. Saliers* (Collegeville, MN: Liturgical Press, 1998), pp. 169–75.

12 Jacques Pohier, *God in Fragments*; cited here from Ann Loades (ed.), *Spiritual Classics from the Late Twentieth Century* (London: Church House Publishing, 1995), p. 153.

13 Cited here from Loades, *Spiritual Classics from the Late Twentieth Century*, p. 154.

14 Cited here from Loades, *Spiritual Classics from the Late Twentieth Century*, p. 155.

15 Alexander Schmemann, *Great Lent: Journey to Pascha* (New York: SVS, 1974), pp. 31–3.

16 See the Doctrine Commission of the Church of England, 'Spirit, Sacraments and Structures', *We Believe in the Holy Spirit* (London: Church House Publishing, 1991), pp. 75–91, for a good example in Anglicanism, and especially the Liturgical Commission, *On the Way* (London: Church House Publishing, 1995) and note the use of the word and imagery of 'journey' in new baptismal rites across the traditions.

17 Haddon Willmer, 'Taking Responsibility: The Future of Christianity in Our Hands', Haddon Willmer (ed.), *20/20 Visions: The Futures of Christianity in Britain* (London: SPCK, 1992), pp. 132–54.

18 Bernard Cooke, *Sacraments and Sacramentality* (Mystic, CT: TwentyThird Publications, 1983), p. 66.

19 Ann Loades, 'Sacrament', Adrian Hastings, Alistair Mason and Hugh Pyper (eds), *The Oxford Companion to Christian Thought* (Oxford: Oxford University Press, 2000), pp. 634–7.

20 *Common Worship: Services and Prayers for the Church of England* (London: Church House Publishing, 2000), p. 237.

21 Thomas C. Oden, *Pastoral Theology: Essentials of Ministry* (San Francisco: HarperCollins, 1985), p. 175.

22 James F. White, *Christian Worship in North America: A Retrospective* (Collegeville, MN: Liturgical Press, 1997), pp. 312–13.

23 Morton Smith, *Clement of Alexandria and a Secret Gospel of Mark*; cited in Thomas Talley, *The Origins of the Liturgical Year* (Collegeville, MN: Liturgical Press, 1990), pp. 207–8.

24 World Council of Churches, *Baptism, Eucharist and Ministry* (Geneva: World Council of Churches, 1981), Baptism, paragraph 2.

25 Judith Martin, *Miss Manners' Guide to Excruciatingly Correct Behaviour*, cited here from Robert Baker, Larry Nyberg, and Victoria Tufano (eds), *A Baptism Sourcebook* (Chicago, IL: Liturgy Training Publications, 1993), p. 3.

26 *Gathering for Worship: Patterns and Prayers for the Community of Disciples* (Norwich: Canterbury Press, 2005), p. 127.

27 *Baptism, Eucharist and Ministry* Baptism, paragraph 12.

28 *Baptism, Eucharist and Ministry*, Baptism, paragraph 12 (commentary).

29 David R. Holeton (ed.), *Growing in Newness of Life: Christian Initiation in Anglicanism Today* (Toronto, Ont.: Anglican Book Centre, 1993), principle a (p. 229).

30 *Common Worship*, p. 352.

31 Elaine Ramshaw, 'How Does the Church Baptize Infants and Small Children?', Gordon Lathrop (ed.), *What Is Changing in Baptismal Practice?* (Minneapolis, MN: Fortress Press, 1995), pp. 6–13.

32 Ramshaw, 'How Does the Church Baptize . . .?', p. 13.

33 *The Book of Common Order* quoted here from Gordon Wakefield, *An Outline of Christian Worship* (Edinburgh: T & T Clark, 1998), p. 187; cf. *The Methodist Worship Book*, pp. 67–8, and *Common Worship*, p. 359.

34 *Common Worship: Pastoral Services* (London: Church House Publishing, 2000), p. 1.

35 Philip Pfatteicher, *Liturgical Spirituality* (Valley Forge, PA: Trinity Press International, 1997), p. 241.

36 Quoted here from in William C. Platcher, *Narratives of a Vulnerable God: Christ, Theology and Scripture* (Louisville: Westminster John Knox Press, 1993), p. 143.

37 *The Methodist Worship Book*, pp. 73–4.

38 *Common Worship*, p. 49; cf. *The Promise of His Glory: For the Season from All Saints to Candlemas* (London: Church House Publishing, 1991): 'The water may be sprinkled over the people, or placed in vessels by the door for them to make the Sign of the Cross as they leave, or poured out over the threshold' (p. 221).

39 Richard Giles, *Creating Uncommon Worship: Transforming the Liturgy of the Eucharist* (Norwich: Canterbury Press, 2004), p. 100.

40 Giles, *Creating Uncommon Worship*, p. 101.

41 Giles, *Creating Uncommon Worship*, p. 102.

42 Regina Kuehn, *A Place for Baptism* (Chicago, IL: Liturgy Training Publications, 1990); Jermone Overbeck, *Ancient Fonts, Modern Lessons* (Chicago, IL: Liturgy Training Publications, 1998); Anita Stauffer, *On Baptismal Fonts: Ancient and Modern* (Nottingham: Grove Books, 1994).

43 Quoted here from Graham Kings and Geoff Morgan, *Offerings from Kenya to*

Anglicanism: Liturgical Tests and Contexts including 'A Kenyan Service of Holy Communion' (Cambridge: Grove Books, 2001), p. 34.

44 *Common Worship*, p. 55.

45 *Common Worship*, p. 152.

46 Louis Weil, *A Theology of Worship* (Cambridge, MA: Cowley, 2002), pp. 8–9.

47 'O Blessed Spring' © Susan Palo Cherwein, found in *Wonder, Love and Praise: A Supplement to the Hymnal 1982* (New York: Church Publishing, 1997), no. 765.

48 Michael Perham, *New Handbook of Pastoral Liturgy* (London: SPCK, 2000), p. 163.

49 Gordon W. Lathrop, 'Afterword', Gordon W. Lathrop (ed.), *What Is Changing in Baptismal Practice?* (Minneapolis, MN: Fortress Press, 1995), pp. 30–1.

Chapter 7 Liturgy and the Fulness of Life: Liturgical Spirituality

1 Ann Loades, 'Why Worship?', *In Illo Tempore* (2000), pp. 16–24.

2 J. D. Critchton, 'A Theology of Worship', Cheslyn Jones, Edward Yarnold, Geoffrey Wainwright and Paul Bradshaw (eds), *The Study of Liturgy* (London: SPCK, 1992), pp. 3–31.

3 Loades, 'Why Worship?', p. 17.

4 Critchton, 'A Theology of Worship', p. 9.

5 Loades, 'Why Worship?', p. 17.

6 Daniel W. Hardy and David F. Ford, *Jubilate: Theology in Praise* (London: Darton, Longman and Todd, 1984), p. 9.

7 Hardy and Ford, *Jubilate*, p. 1.

8 Hardy and Ford, *Jubilate*, p. 6.

9 Hardy and Ford, *Jubilate*, p. 7.

10 David F. Ford and Alistair I. McFadyen, 'Praise', Peter H. Sedgwick (ed.), *God in the City: Essays and Reflections for the Archbishop of Canterbury's Urban Theology Group* (London: Mowbray, 1995), pp. 95–104.

11 *New Patterns for Worship* (London: Church House Publishing, 2002), pp. 443–8.

12 Frank Henderson, *Liturgies of Lament* (Chicago, IL: Liturgy Training Publications, 1992).

13 Michael Downey, *Worship at the Margins: Liturgy and Spirituality* (Washington, DC: Pastoral Press, 1991), pp. 224–5.

14 David Power, *The Eucharistic Mystery: Revitalizing the Tradition* (New York: Crossroad, 1992), p. 337.

15 Private correspondence.

16 Andy Raine and John Skinner of the Northumbria Community (eds), *Celtic Daily Prayer: A Northumbrian Office* (London: HarperCollins, 1994), pp. 21–2.

17 *Modern Services: Morning Prayer, Evening Prayer, Baptism*, etc. (Nairobi: Uzima Press, 1994), p. 8.

18 Aidan Kavanagh, *On Liturgical Theology* (Collegeville, MN: Liturgical Press, 1984), p. 153.

19 Kavanagh, *On Liturgical Theology*, p. 153.

20 Kavanagh, *On Liturgical Theology*, p. 153.

21 Kavanagh, *On Liturgical Theology*, p. 168.

22 Kavanagh, *On Liturgical Theology*, p. 176.

23 Kavanagh, *On Liturgical Theology*, p. 175.

24 Gordon Lathrop, 'Liturgy and Mission in a North American Context', Thomas H. Schattauer (ed.), *Inside out: Worship in an Age of Mission* (Minneapolis, MN: Fortress Press, 1999), pp. 201–12.

25 Lathrop, 'Liturgy and Mission', p. 203. The point parallels David Ford's: 'We could imagine having someone else as the focus of our life who would narrow our attention and limit our concerns. But to concentrate on the face of Jesus Christ is to find our boundaries shifting and expanding as we slowly "grasp what is the breadth and length and height and depth of Christ's love". This is someone whose hospitality is universal – face by face by face. To be before his face is to find that he is looking with love on all sorts of unexpected, marginalized or to us disagreeable people, as well as on us. Wherever he is he brings them as part of his community. So we find our heart is overwhelmed in new ways by those to whom his gaze, words and actions direct us' (*The Shape of Living* [London: Fount, 1997], p. 22).

26 Robert Hovda, *Strong, Loving and Wise: Presiding in Liturgy* (Collegeville, MN: Liturgical Press, 1976), p. 18.

27 Robert Hovda, 'The Vesting of Liturgical Ministers', John H. Baldovin (ed.), *Robert Hovda: The Amen Corner* (Collegeville, MN: Liturgical Press, 1994), pp. 213–33.

28 Hovda, 'Vesting of Liturgical Ministers', p. 220.

29 Hovda, *Strong, Loving and Wise*, p. 19.

30 Don E. Saliers, *Worship as Theology: Foretaste of Glory Divine* (Nashville, TN: Abingdon Press, 1994), p. 145.

31 Saliers, *Worship as Theology*, p. 213.

32 Saliers, *Worship as Theology*, p. 15.

33 Don E. Saliers, *Worship Come to Its Senses* (Nashville, TN: Abingdon Press, 1996), p. 30.

34 E. Bryon Anderson, 'Linking Liturgy and Life', E. Byron Anderson (ed.), *Worship Matters: A United Methodist Guide to Ways of Worship*, Volume 1 (Nashville, TN: Discipleship Resources, 1999), pp. 63–9.

35 Anderson, 'Linking Liturgy and Life', p. 67.

36 Don E. Saliers, *The Soul in Paraphrase: Prayer and the Religious Affections* (Akron, OH: Order of St Luke, 1991), p. 80.

37 Saliers, *Worship as Theology*, p. 134.

38 *United Methodist Worship Book* (Nashville, TN: United Methodist Publishing House, 1989), p. 446.

39 Anderson, 'Linking Liturgy and Life', p. 68.

40 Anderson, 'Linking Liturgy and Life', p. 68.

41 Anderson, 'Linking Liturgy and Life', p. 69.

42 Don E. Saliers, *Worship and Spirituality* (Akron, OH: Order of St Luke, 1996), pp. 67–8.

43 Saliers, *Worship and Spirituality*, p. 68.

Conclusion: Presiding in Liturgy

1 William Seth Adams, *Shaped by Images: One who Presides* (New York: Church Publishing, 1995) p. 27.

2 *Sacrosanctum concilium* 14. Austin Flannery (ed.), *Vatican Council II: Conciliar and Post-Conciliar Documents* (New York: Costello, 1975).

3 Robert Hovda, *Strong, Loving and Wise* (Collegeville, MN: Liturgical Press, 1976), p. 13.

4 James F. White, 'Shaping the 1972 United Methodist Eucharistic Rite', *Christian Worship in North America: A Retrospective* (Collegeville, MN: Liturgical Press, 1997), pp. 143–53.

5 James Empereur, *Worship: Exploring the Sacred* (Washington, DC: Pastoral Press, 1987), pp. 161–83.

6 Empereur, *Worship: Exploring the Sacred*, p. 173.

7 Richard Giles, 'The Making of a Cathedral', John Ander Runkle (ed.), *Searching for Sacred Space: Essays on Architecture and Liturgical Design in the Episcopal Church* (New York: Church Publishing, 2002), pp. 183–204.

8 Empereur, *Worship: Exploring the Sacred*, p. 172.

9 John Hughes, *The Pastor's Notebook* (Eastbourne: Kingsway, 2003), pp. 153–55.

10 Robert Hovda, 'Liturgy Forming Us in the Christian Life', Eleanor Bernstein (ed.), *Liturgy and Spirituality in Context: Perspectives on Prayer and Culture* (Collegeville, MN: Liturgical Press, 1990), pp. 136–50.

11 Stories related from experience of worship at St Patrick, Atlanta, 1998; St Barnabas, Cambridge, 1995.

Acknowledgements and Sources

The author and publisher are grateful to the various authors and publishers who have kindly granted permission for their copyrighted material to be used in this book.

'As Newborn Stars' by Carl P Daw. Word copyright © 1968 Hope Publishing Company, administered by CopyCare PO Box 77, Haliham, BN27 3EF UK music@copycare.com Used by permission.

Material from *The Book of Common Prayer* (1979) of the Episcopal Church of the United States of America is in the public domain.

Material from *Common Worship: Services and Prayer for the Church of England* is © 2000 Archbishop's Council. Used by permission.

'Litany to a Dark God' is © Nicola Slee. Used by permission of Nicola Slee and SPCK.

The prayer, 'Lord, you have always given strength for the coming day' is © Churches Together in Britain and Ireland, and was written for the Week of Prayer for Christian Unity 1988. Used by permission.

A Psalm from *The Manhattan Psalter* is © 2002 Liturgical Press. Used by permission.

A Psalm from *The Message Psalms* is © NavPress. Used by permission.

Material from *The Methodist Worship Book* is © 1999 Trustees for Methodist Church Purposes. Used by permission of Methodist Publishing House.

Material from *Modern Services* is © 1991, 1994 (Anglican) Church of the Province of Kenya. Used by permission.

Index of Select Names and Subjects